God-Man The Word Made Flesh

God-Man The Word Made Flesh

George Carey

CONTENTS

THE REVOLUTIONARY PLANET, URANOUS, ENTERED THE

THE hour has struck that opens the door for a New Dispensation for man, and the standing prophecy, proclaimed, trumpet-tongued, down thru the ages, **is**

n ow being fulfilled.   The old order is dying "Amidst **its** worshippers."

God's loosened thunders shake the world! Across the lurid sky the-war birds scream! Earth's millions die!

Fear and woe unutterable!

The fires of purification are lighted!

Into the cosmic melting pot has been cast hate, race prejudice, self-ishness and the devils of greed !

The towers of superstition and tyranny are falling!

The thrones and scepters of kings lie scattered and crushed along the highway of nations!

Pride has fallen from its insecure pinnacle of shame I

The rich are terror stricken!

"Their silver has been cast into the street!" "Their gold has been re-moved from them!"

"The merchants of the earth weep and mourn, for no man buyeth their merchandise I"

The churches are in panic! The liquor power rages I

The gambler is terror stricken !

The grafting politician seeks a hiding place and finds none I

The briber flees when "no man pursueth !"

The priest and preacher pray, but no help comes, for they, too, must be judged!

The harlot alone seems unafraid, BECAUSE SHE IS NOT A HYP-OCRITE, and has heard the words, "The harlots will enter the kingdom before you I"

Mankind has gone to the limit of animalism I

THE SOUL WALKS FORTH, NAKED AND ASHAMED. IT IS HIGH NOON OF THE JUDGMENT DAY.

-Written in 1916.

REDEMPTION, THE ULTIMATE GOAL OF HUMANITY

TAOISM: "Man consisting of a trinity of spirit, mind and body, cometh forth from the Eternal, and after putting off *desire* re-enters the glory of Tao."

Brahmanism: "Man's inner self is one with the self of the Universe, and to that Universe and to that Unity it must return in the fullness of time."

Buddhism: "Man, fundamentally Divine, is held in the three worlds by *desire*. Purification from *desire* leads the man to Nirvana."

Hebrewism: "Man came into being through emanation from the will of the King, therefore is divine."

Egyptian: "Teaches the divinity of man, Osiris as his source."

Zoroastrianism: "Man is a spark of the universal flame to be ultimately united with its source."

Orphic: "Man has in him potentially the sum and sub stance of the Universe."

- Christian: "Man made in the image of God-Body, Soul and Spirit-a Trinity."

THE KINGDOM AT HAND

MAN is within one step of his ideal-the ultimate goal of his de-sires-that realm of freedom where he will rio longer be subject to law, but, being

"led by the spirit," will realize that he, himself, is an operator and at-tribute of the law.

Man is law in action. Will man now take the final step into complete liberty and become a god, or continue to eat of the husks of sJual con-cept and still cower beneath the lash of "precedent'and authority"?

There is no "salvation" or regeneration for Man, as long as he believes in vicarious atonement. The man who needs saving by that process is not worth the price.

Recognition of eternal unity will save Man from the idea that he needs saving, because it will reconcile him to his- place and mission in the Plan-the Great Necessity. It will reveal to him his true kinship to the causeless cause, the beginningless beginning, and he will know that he is an attribute of universal energy from which all forms, thoughts, mo-tions, sounds, colors, and so-called "good and evil," proceed.

In the full light of this wisdom, man will not search for personal saviors, nor quibble about the meaning of the words of men who died tho1,1sands of years ago.

Jesus, Christ, Truth, Life-forever preaches the ser mon in the ear of man: "Lo I I am with you now." **He** that confesseth not that Jesus Christ *is* come in the flesh, the same is an Anti-Christ."

Only the spiritually blind look for the "coming" of Truth, or Life, the Christ who is ever present, or for the "coming" of a kingdom which is already at hand. "When ye pray for a thing know that ye have it now."

If we accept a certain statement uttered, as an ultima tum, by some one who lived in the dim past, we may be called upon to reconcile the utterance with another opin

i on, spoken or written by the same person, which seems to contradict previous statements in which we have placed our trust.

These persons, bdng dead, cannot be asked for an ex planation in regard to the seeming contradiction. If they could, they might respond, as Walt Whitman did when a critic hinted that the "good gray poet" contradicted him self: "Do I contradict myself? Then I contradict my self. I am large, I contain multitudes."

We must consider the facts that the opinions uttered by men in past ages extend over a period of years, during which time empires rose and fell, and new concepts of life, due to planetary and zodiacal changes, obtained rec ognition. Thus radical changes occurred in the social, religious, scientific and industrial world.

Viewing the question in this light, need we wonder that the_seers and sages, saints and scientists of the past should sometimes contradict themselves?

Are we, today, so very consistent?

Do we not enact what we call "sacred laws," immedi ately violate them and carry the case to the court of last resort and get the "sacred" law repealed?

We have had high and low tariff, bimetalism and gold standard, and our great statesmen valiantly upheld the

·free coinage of silver in the year 1895, and in 1896 these same captains of finance declared through the public press that free coinage of silver would destroy civiliza tion, tear down the pillars of Hercules and wrench the stars from their cosmic thrones.

We have contradicted ourselves in our opinion of the earth's shape, the distance to the Sun, the origin and oper ation of electricity, the cause of light, the divisibility of elemental gases, the circulation of the blood, the reality of hell and the devil and other subjects too numerous to men- tion.

Then, shall we forever wrangle over the contradictory statements of dead men who wrought in their day as best they might with the light and data at their com mand, with no thought that people in future ages would war to the death or live with hate in their hearts for

[12]

their fellows who differ with them on baptism, the size of Noah's ark, or whether a prophet swallowed a fish or a fish swallowed a prophet?

So much for the old world belief, that the Scriptures (writings) are records of men and women and places, geographical, historical, etc.

These wonderful statements are fables, parables, alle gories, dealing with the chemical, physiological, anatom ical and astrological opera- tions of the HUMAN BODY, "Fearfully and /Wonderfully made."

"Great are the symbols of Being,

But that which is symboled is greater; Vast the create and beheld,

But vaster the llward *Creator.*"-*Richard Real/.*

4

BOOKS REJECTED BY THE
COUNCIL OF NICEA, AND OTHER

BOOKS of the Koran-Persia; Hebrew (Meaning Passover) ; Esther; Solomon; Egyptian Book of the Dead; Adam; Eve; Enoch; Seth; Seventh Book of Moses; St. Thomas (The Doubter); Nicodemus; Ptah

Hotep, the oldest book known; The Kabballah.

Again, the researches of such theological scholars as James Legge, L.L.D., first Professor of Chinese, at Ox ford University; Prof. Wm. Jennings, P.H.D., and Hon. Clement Allen of the Royal Asiatic Society, beside several hundred who might be named, embracing the leaders of thought along lines of "original sources," all agree that hundreds, if not thousands, of ancient manuscripts, tablets and carvings indubitably prove that all races of all people that have ever inhabited the earth have striven, as best they could, to leave records of the chemistry and physi ol-ogy of their own bodies.

Science, Egyptology, Inda-Iranian, Chinese, Japanese, Persian, or Sanskrit, all, all, forever strove to solve the riddle of the human body.

Seven hundred years **B. C.** we have the Shu King, China's oldest book; The Shih King, 600 B. C.; The Yi King, 1143 B. C.

Then came Confucius, 551-478 **B. C.**

The writings, statements, philosophy and symbols of these witnesses of the truth of being corroborates our 66 witnesses in every detail.

The writers of this book have in their possession a library of the ancient scriptures referred to above and know whereof they speak; but, as printing and book mak ing is well nigh prohibited by cost, we feel that we are not justified in lengthy quotations. Again, nothing really new can be added after the *ne plus ultra* statement, "There is *no* other way under heaven whereby ye may be

[**14**]

saved except Jesus, Christed and crucified."

However, for the information of our readers we will give the table of contents of Vol. 14 of the Sacred Books and Early Literature of the East, entitled "The Great Rejected Books":

OLD TESTAMENT APOCRYPHA

1. The Books of Adam and Eve; The lives of Adam and Eve; The Appcalypse of Moses; The Slavonic Book of Eve.
2. The Writings Attributed to Enoch; The Great Prophetic Book of Enoch; The Lost Book of Noah.
3. The Apocalypse of Baruch; His Vision of Heaven.
4. The Story of Ahikar;

The Old Armenian Version; The New-found Ancient Book.

THE   NEW   TESTAMENT APOCRYPHA

5. The Gospels of Christ's Childhood;

The Protevangelium, or Original Gospel of James; Gospel of Thomas the Doubter;

The Gospel of Pseudo-Matthew; An Arabic Gospel of the Infancy.

6. The Gospels of Nicodemus;

The Greek Gospel of Nicodemus; A Later Gospel;
The Harrowing of Hell; The Acts of Pilate;
The Letters of Pilate.

NAMES

NAMES will be explained without alphabetical order, the object being to show that the 66 books of the *whole book* (Holy Book), were 66 statements by

66 different writers about the same identical subject-the *human body*, its chemical operation and the planetary positions, impinging to create and bring into physical manifestation the visible universe.

ADAM: Red earth, or flow of spirit or energy, dammed up.

EVE: Mother of all the living; ether or pure spirit; Mother of God-Water; fluid; esse.

CAIN: What is gotten-acquisition, a spear, a smith; a worker.

ABEL: Transitoriness; breath; vapor; moisture (ab- sorbed-killed by Cain).

SETH: Seed, seedling or germ. MAN: See Adam.

WoMAN: Wom(b)an, or womb in man (mankind); the regenerative womb or manger in the solar plexus. (See Bethlehem, house-of-bread).

Non: Flight; Cain absorbed (killed) Abel (moisture) and vegetation sprang up (shoot-movement).

WIFE: Marriage of earth and water.

JOSHUA: Jehovah-in-salvation; son of Nun-fish. MosEs: Drawn from the water; fish.

ABRAM: High father, father of elevation. ABRAHAM: Father of a multitude.

AARON: Enlightened (Buddha-Third Eye).

HoR: Mountain, Mountain of Aaron, situated on the East side of the great valley of the Arabah, the high est and most conspicuous of the whole range of the sandstone mountains of Edom, having close beneath it on its East side, the mysterious city of Petra.

PETRA: Rock; Rock city, south of Jericho. EDOM: Red; Edom or Odumea-pituitary body.

JACOB: Circle; heel-catcher; lier-in-wait. (Applied *to* the 12 Zodiacal signs, in astrology; to the solar plexus, in physiology.)

LEAH: First wife of Jacob, represented in astrology by several of the Zodiacal signs, namely: Reuben, libra; Simeon, Scorpio; Levi, Sagittarius; Judah, Capricorn; Issachar, Gemini; Zebulum, Cancer, and Dinah, Leo. The name means, in Hebrew, wearied, weak, slow action, inferior. (See cut.)

RACHEL: .,. Second wife of Jacob: a ewe; Mother of Jo seph and Benjamin, represented in astrology by Vir go for Joseph; ijenjamin having a deeply esoteric significance. It represents the product.

BENJAMIN: Son of the right hand; son of my old age; called first, by his mother, "son of my sorrow." He was the only child to be born in Palestine-the Holy Land. In Smith's Bible Dictionary we find this, "The Ark was in Benjamin." To esoteric students this statement is significant. Plainly speaking, Ben jamin is the same as Jesus and refers to the seed or son that redeems.

PALESTINE: Land of sojourners; country of Israel or Holy Land.

ARARAT: Holy Land. ABBA: Father (God). ABSALOM: Father of Peace.

ADAH, ADAIAH, ADDI: Ornament, whom God has adorned: Refers to Pituitary body.

ADONAI: Lord.

ZoHELETH: THE STONE; serpent, the rolling stone; the serpent stone, the stone of the conduit.

G1LGAL: A circle or rolling away; the place where the 12 stones were set up, the place of the "Passover," "A hot depressed district," says Smith's Bible Dic tionary. Refers in anatomy to the 12th dorsal ver tebra, at which place the semi-lunar ganglion con nects. At this point the seed or ark enters Jordan or the spinal cord.

JORDAN: The descender; the flowing river. A river that has never been navigable, flowing into a sea that has never known a port. About 200 miles long, rising from the roots of Anti-Lebanon to the head of the Dead Sea. "The river of God"-see Smith's Bible Dictionary. In anatomy-the *Spinal cord,* the great nerve which is supplied with fluid from the claustrum in the cerebrum.

"The Jordan was crossed over by Joshua (Fish) , the son of Nun (fish)," Smith's Bible Dictionary. As Joshua and Jesus mean the same, we see by this that this is the place of the baptism of Jesus. See further refer ence to this.

Only two fords are mentioned in the Bible. These in anatomy are the end of the spinal cord at the 12th Dorsal vertebra, and at the base of the skull.

Smith also says that the true source of the Jordan is "Underground in Phiala (meaning vial or bowl), and on the *right hand* side." "It is from this 'cave' that the Jordan commences its course above ground." Com pare this description with the anatomy of the head and its meaning be comes clear. Smith tells us that the upper part of the slope is alive with bursting fountains and gushing streams that find their way into the Jor dan. These in Anatomy refer to the glands in the brain that connect with the spinal cord. Read in Smith's Bible Dictionary the wonderful de scription ,of this River.

GENESARETH: Gardens of the Prince; a crescent shaped (Moon-shaped) plain on the western shore of Lake Genesareth, which is also the Sea of Galilee. The Sea of Galilee is the semi-lunar ganglion thru which the seed or Jesus passes to reach the spinal cord. The Jordan enters in at the North and passes out at th·esouth. It *abounds in fish.*

DAUGHTER: Bath. Anything regarded as feminine. GALILEE: A circle or circuit.

NAZARETH: Shoot, sprout, twig.

CAPERNAUM: Village of Nahum (consolation). CANA: Place of reeds; Lungs.

JERICHO: Place of fragrance; Cerebellum.

JOURNEY OF JOSEPH AND MARY

T HE MARVELOUS STORY OF THE JOURNEY OF JOSEPH AND MARY TO JERUSALEM TO PAY THEIR TAXES PHYSIOLOGICALLY EXPLAINED

ON EITHER side of the Thalamus, in the head, is a gland, known in physiology as the Pineal, on the posterior, and the Pituitary on the anterior side of

the Thalamus.

The Pineal is cone shaped, and secretes a yellow or golden fluid. The Pituitary Body, opposite it, is ellipsoid in shape, and contains a whitish secretion, like milk.

The fluids that are found in both these bodies come from the same source, namely, the Claustrum, which means "barrier" or "cloister," and is referred to as cloister for the very good reason that a precious and holy thing is secreted or secluded there. Saint Claus, or Santa Claus, is another term for this precious fluid, which is indeed a holy gift in the body of each one of us.

The precious fluid which flows down from the Claus trum separates, part going into the Pineal gland and part to the Pituitary body, and these, being special laboratories of the head, differentiate the fluid from the Claustrum, and it takes on the colors above mentioned, and in the Pineal Gland becomes yellow and has electric properties. The Pituitary Body, having the milk-like fluid, has mag netic properties.

These two glands are the male and female, the Joseph and Mary of the physical body, and are the par ents of the spiritual son born in the solar plexus of each human being, commencing about the age of twelve.

This yellow and white material, which is the milk and honey referred to in the Bible, the children of Israel having been given the promise of a return to this land flowing with milk and honey, at last reaches the solar plexus via semi-lunar ganglia (see ch rt), the Bethle-

hem of the physical body. In Hebrew, Bethlehem means "house" (Beth) of bread (lehem). "I am the bread of life," said the allegorical Jesus.

In the solar plexus is a thimble-shaped depression-a CAVE-or manger, and in this is deposited the psycho physical seed, or holy child, born of this immaculate con ception. This psycho-physical seed is also called "fish," as it has the odor of fish and is formed in the midst of the waters, the pure water. "Jesus is a fish in the midst of the waters"-St. Augustine. Before birth the human foetus floats, like a fish, in the fluids by which it is sur rounded. And as it is with the child formed on the generative plane, so it is with the spiritual child born in the solar-plexus-the Bethlehem. Joseph and Mary, by furnishing the material for the spiritual child which was to redeem the child or body formed in generation, paid the symbolical redemption money.

Holy Ghost-Greek for breath. The breath, descend ing the *pneumogastric* nerve *into* the solar center, enters the manger where Joseph and Mary are, and where is Jesus the Seed *literally "conceived by the Holy Ghost."*

MAN

"God hath made man upright; but they have sought out many inventions."

THERE is an automatic procedure within the human body, which, *if not interfered with* will do away with sickness, trouble, sorrow and death, as stated

in the Bible

Truly, mankind, or the natural man, seeks many ways and means to prevent the upright, perfect, automatic way from "accomplishing that whereunto it was sent."

The natural man forever seeks pleasurable sensation, wn1ch is at enmity with God. Physical sensation (the "Pleasures of sin for a season," or limited duration, re.:

£erred to by Paul, are under the law, or below the solar olexus, hence, "He that is *led by the spirit* is not under the **J.:i.w.**"

The 21st letter of the Hebrew alphabet, "schin" or "shin," lacks one of the complete alphabet, "tav," the 22nd letter, meaning the "cross."

Herewith are given a few of the Greek and Hebrew

<:haracters that have been translated, "sin, or falling

<ihort." Hebrew: "asham, het, chet, hata, avon" (trans lated iniquity more than 200 times), means "Conceived in sin and brought forth in iniquity" (or sin), oesha or pasha.

In Greek we find this word written as "harmartia, proanartano, anamartetos, anomia, anomos, parabaimo." Any act, coming under the meaning of sin, retards or prevents the automatic action of the seed, which, if not interfered with, *lifts up a portion* (one-tenth) of the life essence (oil or secretion) that constantly flows down the spinal cord (a *"Strait* and narrow way") and trans mutes it, thus increasing its power many fold and per petuating the body indefinitely, or until the Ego desires tc,

dissolve it by rates of motion set in action by its inherent will.

If the allegories of Matthew, Mark, Luke and John, as well as Paul's Epistles and Acts of the Apostles teach any thing, they teach the mastery and transmutation of the human body by anyone who obeys the physiological guide book-the *whole* book-the Holy Bible.

But let the reader observe that each of the 66 books, as well as an almost countless number of ancient books of all races and languages, teach the same mathematical and physiological facts.

Man has turned the mighty power he possesses to every object and principle of force in the universe except *himself,* the greatest miracle of all. When man focuses his divine thinking lens upon himself, he will realize that he is an epitome of unlimited Cosmic Energy. Then the "Heavens will roll together as a scroll" and reveal the Real Man as "the Lamb of God that taketh away the sins of the world."

IT: THE ETERNITY OF PERFECTION

A CHILD brought to its mother a piece of ice and asked: "What is this?"

The mother answered, "it is ice."

Again the child asked, "What is there in ice?" The mother answered: "There is water in the ice."

The child desired to find the water in the ice, and it procured a hammer, pounded the piece of ice into little bits and the warm air soon changed all the ice to water. The child was grievously disappointed, for the ice that the child supposed contained water had disappeared.

And the child said, "Where is the ice that contained this water?"

And so it came to pass that the mother was compelled, by the child's persistent questions, to say, "ice is all water; there is no such thing as ice; that which we call ice is crystalized or frozen water."

The child understood.

A student brought to his teacher some water and asked, "What is water? What does it contain?"

The teacher answered, "Water contains oxygen and hydrogen," and then explained how the two gases might be separated and set free by heat.

The student boiled the water until all of the molecules of oxygen and hydrogen had been set free, but he was surprised to find that all of the water had disappeared.

Then the student asked of the teacher, "Where is the water that held the gases that have escaped?"

Then was the teacher compelled by the student's per sistent questions to answer, "Water itself is the product of oxygen and hydrogen. Water does not contain any thing other than these gases. In reality, there is no such substances or fluid as water; that which we name water is a rate of motion set in operation by the union of two

[23]

P arts of hydrogen with one part of oxygen and, of course, the phenomenon disappears when the union of the gases is broken."
The student understood.

A devout scientist presented himself before God and said, "Lord, what are these gases men call oxygen and hydrogen?"

The good Lord answered and said, "They are mole cules in the blood and body of the universe."

Then spake the scientist, "Lord, wilt thou tell me of the kind of molecules that compose Thy blood and body?" The Lord replied, "These same molecules, gases or principles, compose my blood and body; for I and the

universe are one and the same."

Once again the scientist said, "My Lord, may I ask, then, what is spirit and what is matter?"

And thus answered the Lord:

"As ice and water are one, and the gases and water are one, so is spirit and matter one. The different phases and manifestations cognized by man in the molecules of My body-that is, the universe-are caused by the Word; thus, they are My thoughts clothed with form."

Now the scientist felt bold, being redeemed from fear, and asked "is my blood, then, identical with Thy blood in composition and Divine Essence?"

And the Lord said, "Yea, thou art one with the Father."

The scientist now understood and said:

"Now mine eyes are opened and I perceive that, when I eat, I partake of Thy body; when I drink, I drink of Thy blood; and when I breathe, I breathe Thy spirit."

So-called matter is Pure Intelligence and nothing else because there is not anything else.

Pure intelligence cannot progress or become better. There is nothing but Intelligence. Omnipresence, Omni potence, Omniscience must mean Intelligence; therefore these terms are all included in the word.

Let us adopt a short word that will express all that the above written words are intended to express, namely, the word IT. "I" stand for all-the eternal I. "T" stands

for operation, manifestation, vibration, action or motion. The "I" in motion is "T," or Crossification, viz., the T-cross. We say, "IT" rains I "IT is cold I" "IT is all right I" What do we mean by "It?" Whoknows? Some say, "The weather!" Others, "Natural phenom ena!" Very well, then-what do we mean by "the weather," or "natural phenomena?" Why, just It, of course!

IT does not progress; it does not need to. IT forever manifests, op-erates, differentiates and presents different aspects or viewpoints of IT-SELF. But these different phases are neither good, better nor best, neither bad nor worse-simply different shades and colorings of the One and Only Intelligence.

Every so-called thing, whether it be animal, vegetable or mineral, molecule or atom, ion or electron, is the result of the One Intelligence expressing itself in different rates of motion. Then what is Spirit?

Spirit means breath or life. Spirit, that which is breathed into man, must be intelligence, or man would not be intelligent. Non-intelligent substance, which is, of course, unthinkable, would not breathe into any-thing, nor make it intelligent if it did. Therefore, we see that Spirit, In-telligence and Matter are one and the same Esse in different rates of motion.

So-called molecules, atoms, electrons, know what to do. They know where and how to cohere, unite and operate to form a leaf or a flower. They know how to separate and distintegrate that same leaf or flower. These particles of omnipresent life build planets, suns and systems; they hurl the comet on its way across measureless deserts of star-dust and emboss its burning path.

From the materialistic and individual concept of life and its operations, it is pitiable and pathetic to view the wrecks along the shores of science. It is only when we view these apparently sad failures from the firm foothold of the unity of being and the operation of wisdom that we clearly see in these frictions and warring elements and temoorary defeats and victories the chemical operation of Eternal Spirit-operating with its *own substance-its* very

Self. It is only through the fires of transmutation that we are enabled to see that all life is one Eternal Life and therefore cannot be taken, injured, or destroyed.

The fitful, varying, changing beliefs of men in the tran sition stage from the sleep and dreams of materialism to the realization of the Oneness of Spirit show forth in a babel of words and theories, a few of which I shall briefly consider, beginning with the yet popular belief in Evolu tion:

The evolutionary concept has its starting point in the idea (a) that matter-so-called-is a something separate from mind, intelligence, or Spirit; (b) that this matter had a beginning; (c) that it contains within itself the desire to progress or improve; and, finally, that th race is progressing, becoming wiser, better, etc.

Against this assumption, I submit the proposition that the Universe-one verse-always existed without begin ning or ending and is and always has been absolutely per fect in all its varied manisfestations and operations.

A machine is no stronger than its weakest part. If the self-existing universe is weak or imperfect in any part, it must, of necessity, always have been so. Having all the knowledge there *is-being* all-it is unthinkable that there is any imperfection anywhere. Everything we see, feel, or taste, or in any manner sense, is perfect substance, con densed or manifested from perfect elements, but all differ in their notes, vibrations, or modes or rates of motion. A serpent is as perfect, therefore as good, as a man. With out feet, it outruns a man; with_out hands, it outclimbs the ape, and has been a symbol of wisdom through all the ages. Man is an evil thing to the serpent's consciousness. Neither are evil-nor good. They are different expres sions or variations of the "Play of the Infinite Will."

The brain of the jelly-fish is composed of the same ele ments, of the same substance as the brain of a man, merely of a different combination. Can man tell what the jelly fish is thinking, or why it moves and manifests its energy thus or so? How, then, is man wiser than the jelly-fish because his thoughts are of a different nature and operate to different ends?

Wisdom-all there is-simply operates, manifests, ex presses forms, or creates them, of, self-existing sub stance. As wisdom is without beginning or end, so are all its operations or manifestations without beginning or end.

Modern man is now taking his first lessons in con densing or materializing air, while through unnumbered ages the spider has performed the miracle without the necessity of first attending a school of chemistry. The *modus operandi* by which the spider forms his web from air is the desp'air of science. The wisdom of the ant or beaver strikes dumb all the believers in the Darwinian dream. The perfect co-operative commonwealth of the bees is still the unattained ideal of man.

Beneath the soil upon which falls the shadow of the throne of Menelik, tlie Abyssinian King, are layers and strata of buried civilizations, and astronomers in China mapped the Heavens, named the stars, calculated the eclipses and the return of comets ages before Moses led the Hebrews out of bondage, or the walls of Baalbeck cast a shade for the Arab and his camel.

The evidences and witnesses of the wisdom of men on earth hundreds of thousands of years ago confront the scientific investigator at every turn. Here the Rosseta Stone, and there the Inscribed Cylinder of Arioch or Statue of Gudea, King of Chaldea. Prophecies, inscribed on Cunieform tablets of Clay, foretelling the building of the Pyramids, are brought to light by the excavator; and the history of the Chinese Empire, running back in links of an unbroken chain for one hundred and fifty thousand years, forever refute the theory of the "Descent of Man I" Side by side with the anscient Asiatics, who knew all that we today know, dwelt the Crystal, the Cell, the Jelly-fish, the Saurian, the Ape and the Cave-Man. Side by side with the masons, who could build arches of stone in ancient Yucatan that mock at the ravages of Time, lived and wrought the ant, operating in its co-operative common wealth of which man can still only dream. Side by side with the cave men and cannibals dwells the spider, whose operation in aerial elements is the despair of chemical

I nvestigators. And when Solomon's golden-spired temple illuminated the Holy City, or the tower of Babel grew toward the clouds, or the Mound Builders recorded their history in rock and soil, the eagle and the dove calmly floated in the air and wondered when men would evolve to their plane of science. They are wondering still.

Exponents of the evolutionary theory never tire in quot ing Professor Huxley. One who has not read the writings of this eminent scientist would be led to believe by the statements of his followers that he had positive views on the great question of force and matter. Following is an extract from a letter written by Professor Huxley to Charles Kingsley, under date of May 22nd, 1863, taken from the published letters of Huxley by his son, Leonard:

"I don't know whether Matter is anything distinct from Force. I don't know that atoms are anything but pure myths-'Cogito ergo sum' is to my mind a ridiculous piece of bad logic, all I can say at any time being 'Cogito.' The Latin form I hold to be preferable to the English 'I think,' because the latter asserts the existence of an Ego about which the bundle of phenomena at present address ing you knows nothing. I believe in Hamilton, Mansell and Herbert Spencer, so long as they are destructive, and laugh at their beards as soon as they try to spin their own cobwebs."

"Is this basis of ignorance broad enough for you? If you, theologian, can find as firm footing as 1, man of science, do on this foundation of minus naught-there will be naught to fear for our ever diverging. For you see, I am quite as ready to admit your doctrine that souls secrete bodies as I am the opposite one that bodies secrete souls-simply because I deny the possibility of obtaining any evidence as to the truth or falsehood of either hypo thesis. My fundamental axiom of speculative philosophy is that materialism and spiritualism are opposite poles of the same absurdity-the absurdity of imagining that we knew anything about either spirit or matter."

Huxley admitted that he did not know.

As the appetite craves new chemical combinations of food from day to day, so does mind crave new concepts of

$\mathbf{I}$ nfinite life. The word "Infinite" defines an endless dif ferentiation of concept.

If the Spiritual Consciousness-the "mighty Angel" that the clairvoyant seer, John the Revelator, saw descend ing out of the Heavens-shall carry away the pillars of material evolution, a Temple of Truth divinely fair will spring, Phoenix-like, to take its place. Eyes shall then be opened and ears unstopped. Man will then realize that the so-called lower forms of life are just as complex, won derful and difficult to form as the organism of man-that proto-plasm is as wonderful in any other form as in the gray matter of the human brain, which is only another form of its expression-that the molecular composition of a jelly-fish puzzles the greatest chemist, and the wisdom of a beaver is enough to strike dumb all the believers in the Darwinian fairy -tale.

And has the dream of good and evil any better founda tion than has this one of material evolution? We are here to solve the problems of life, not to evade them; and, to name the mighty operations of Eternal Wisdom, good and evil is simply evading instead of solving.

The universal Principle, Spirit, or God, is impartial. Saint and Sinner are one in the Eternal Mind.   God, or Infinite Life is not in the least injured by so-called good or evil.   The Spiritual Ego is the interested party and must work out its *own* Salvation.   There is no point in the universe better, higher, or nearer God, or the centre, than any other point.   All places are necessary, and no one is favored over any other.   As Huxley well said, "Good and evil are opposite poles of the same absurdity." Good must have evil for its opposite, if it exists at all. He who would realize Being must get rid of the concept of good, as well as the concept of evil. Good and evil are qualifications, and Being does not admit of qualification or grades.   It simply is.   The ideal we call good eternally exists, but its name is wisdom's operations.

Nothing is low or high, good or bad, except to that individual con cept which allows comparison. "Comparisons are odious." Physical Science, so-called, declares in its text-books that light travels from the sun to the earth in eight minutes a distance of about ninety-five million miles. To question

his statement a few years ago meant ostracism from the circle of the elect who knew things. But today the icono clast stands at the gate of the temples of learning and batters at the walls with the hammer of Thor. Fear and trembling seize upon the votaries of material gods as they see evolution, progression, the theories of electricity, light and heat, good and evil, all cast into the crucible of truth for transmutation in the Divine Alchemy of Being, all dissolving as pieces of ice of different sizes and shapes change to water.

The present day chemist, as he begins to tread the soil where stood the ancient alchemist, tells us that light and heat are simply the rates of motion of a substance that does not travel from star to star or from sun to planet, but vibrates *in its place* at rates directed by the Eternal Word. This substance, aerial or etheric, does not travel

-it is everywhere present-the body of omnipresent being. .

Men now dare assert that there is no evidence that the sun is hot, but that there is evidence that the sun is the dynamo of the Solar System and so vibrates the etheric substance that light, heat, cold and gravitation are pro duced-not as entities separate from the universal ele ments, but as results or effects produced by different rates of motion of the molecules of the wire-molecular motion

-or of the air or etheric substance, as in wireless teleg raphy.

Another ancient belief, now obsolete, is the progression of man in a better state of existence after death or cess ation of bodily functions. This idea had its origin in the fallacy that there were grades of goodness in the Divine Mind, and that somehow we are not treated right during earth life, and that, in consequence, we must be rewarded by an easy berth "over there." But we now see quite clearly that the great cause of life and all its operations would be unjust to withhold from its sons and daughters for one moment anything that belonged to them. If the Cause ever does wrong, we see no reason why it should repent and do right. If the Cause ever failed in the least particular to give just dues, it m_ay do so a ain at any

ime. The "better state of existence" mentioned above can only come through wisdom obtained here and now; thus will man "work out his own salvation."

The time was, and not so very long ago, when the recognized scientist believed that there were about seven ty-four elements, indivisible, separate and distinct; but the alchemical iconoclast with his hammer of truth has pulverized the fallacy and remorselessly hammered and pounded the seventy-four faces into one countenance.

For a long time, hydrogen gas, the negative pole of water, was supposed to be indivisible beyond all question; but the present day chemist knows it .is only an expression of yet more subtle molecules back of which, "Standeth God within the shadow keeping watch above His own."

A post-mortem examination of some of the wrecks along the shores of the troubled sea of science discloses a belief that the Ego is an individual, who through knowl edge of its divine origin may draw unto itself all things it may desire I But as fast as the Sleepers awaken they see that each Ego is only "part of one stupendous whole" that does not draw unto its lf anything. That there is no law of attraction for the eternal substance is every where present and each one uses exactly that portion pre pared for him from everlasting unto everlasting.

When the continuity of life was first demonstrated be yond question those who caught the first dispatches from disincarnate spirits sprang forth from their beds of mate rial sleep and with half-opened eyes only saw the great truth through "a glass darkly." Then came a babel of words. They jabbered a jargon that needed translation to be understood. The ideas of progression in earth life that obtained among men was transplanted to the spirit realm and we were told by the votaries of spiritual phil osophy that men and women had great opportunities for progression after leaving the flesh. As the idea of a com mencement of the universe was a common belief among those asleep in material consciousness, being the corner stone of evolution, so the idea obtained that the individual had a commencement in the maternal human laboratory.

As these half-awakened individuals could not comprehend

that an action contrary to their concept of good could possibly be caused by Infinite Intelligence they concluded that the so-called bad actions of men and women were prompted by evil earth-bound spirits. These people many of them-also thought that the main object of the existence of Spirits in the Spirit realm was to gather infor mation about mines and stocks and bonds and lotteries and races and thus assist poor mortals to ret-rich-quick. It was supposed that these spirits were posted in regard to deeds and wills and knew when wealthy relatives would shuffle off the mortal coil or when undesirable wives or husbands would "pass out."

But at last the sun of Truth pierced the darkness and the jargon of selfishness changed to the "New Song." We now clearly see that each spirit is a part or attribute of the One Eternal Spirit-therefore has existed always and that the process of generation deals with flesh clothing, or mask for the spirit in which it performs a necessary part in the creative process. The word "person" is de rived from a Greek word, *Persona,* meaning mask.

We see that the phenomena we have called obsession by evil spirits is God's surgery or dynamic operation in His own temple quite as im- possible for us to understand in our present environment as it is for the child to under stand the wisdom and necessity in the operation of the adept surgeon.

And, finally, we now see and realize fully that Eternal Wisdom with- out beginning or end of days does not prog ress before entering a temple of flesh, while it occupies it, or after it leaves it. All creative or formative proc esses may oroperly be termed operations of wisdom or Eternal Life.

In the unwalled temple of the Now, beneath its roofless dome there is no progression, but a constantly moving panorama forever presenting to consciousness new phases of the absolute.

The men and women who do things take hold of oppor tunities and material that they find all about them now, and operate with them, as- tonishing results following the efforts of all who recognize hat eternal force has use for

t hem NOW to drry out the divine plan. We are all operators or work- men in the divine workshop, and the Divine Intelligence, the eternal IT, made no mistake in placing any of us here, but does insist that we recognize that NOW is the time and Here is the place to do our best. As the Great Cause does not need to first practice on lower forms in order at some future time to attain perfection, we must recognize and practice *being* in the present, instead of *becoming* in the future, for the Eternal Now is all the time there is.

"But," you l say, "your cience has taken away my God, and I know not where you have lain Him." On the contrary, I have brought you to the one true God, "which

was, and is, and evermore shall be."

The fifth verse of the last chapter of the book of Job reads as follows : ,

"I have heard of thee by the hearing of the ear; but now mine eye seeth thee."

The wonderful writings and scientific statements found in that Book of all books, the Christian Bible, were recorded at dates covering thousands of years by men and women who never heard of each other. Some of these teachers lived away back in the age when the Solar System was swinging through the zodiacal sign, Taurus; when Phallic worship prevailed; when the number six was understood as sex, and the creative or formative prin ciple operating through the sex functions was worshiped as the very Holy of Holies. Other teachers, who contrib uted to the knowledge of life and its operations contained in the Bible, lived in the age of Aries, a fire sign, when fire and sun were worshiped as the essence of God; and, as heat, the cause of the phenomenon called fire, cannot be seen, it was a reasonable thing to say that "no one can see God and live." So then, it depends upon the point of view one has of God, or the spirit of things, whether he says, "No one can see God and live," or says, "Now mine *eye* seeth thee I"

The writer of the book named Job must have lived more than eight thousand years ago, even before the Taurian age-symbolized by the Winged Bulls of Nineveh

-which was in the Gemini age, the age of perception and

expression, being an air age.   Let it be understood that an age in this connection means twenty-two hundred years, the period for the Solar System to pass across one of the signs of the zodiac.   In an air age, Egos awaken to their divine heritage, and realize their Godhood.   The writer of Job, then, living in the Gemini or air age, could see God and live. Our Solar System has entered the sign Aquarius, another air sign, and the spiritualized elements so act upon our brain-cells that we are able to understand the teachers of a past air age, and also see God and live. Carlyle, the prince of literary critics, said "The book of Job is the most wonderful and beautiful literary produc tion ever given to the world."   Certainly the scientific truths of astrology and alchemy, and of the Spirit's oper ation in flesh, as set forth in that book, are without a parallel.   The letters J, 0, B, have an oc ult, scientific meaning, I and J are the same IOB meaning the same as JOB. I means the Eternal I. All the Hebrew letters were formed from I.   0 means the universe, without beginning or end, and B means Beth, a body, house, church, or temple; Therefore, GOD, or all, may be dis covered as seen in JOB or IOB. The word, Job, has no reference to a person. The name, or letters of the word, symbolize principle, the same as wisdom, knowledge, in telligence, or Christ, or Buddha. We symbolize the prin ciples of our government in personalities, and picture them in the form of a man or woman, namely, Uncle Sam, or Columbia.   But we do more than that: we put words in their mouth and make them utter speech.   And shall we ignore these facts when dealing with the record of past ages?   One record plainly states that Jesus spake only

in parables.

But let us consider more closely the discovery of God. The numerical value of G.O.D., according to ancient Kabalia, is nine-the all of mathematics-no person is alluded to. If the statement, "I and the Father are one," is true, the "I" must be the Father manifested or ex pressed. As it is not possible *to* conceive of the Father exceot through expression, we must conclude that mani festation in some form of so-called matter is eternal the g-reat necessity-and has therefore always been.

It is quite reasonable to think that some oxygen and hydrogen has eternally existed in gaseous form, some in the combination that causes water and some in the con crete or concentrated form known as ice. Then upon the postulate that Spirit and matter-that is, bodily or mate rial expression-are one, it follows logically that matter, including the physical body or temple of man, is as neces sary to the Father-Mother principle while held in a given rate of activity or expression as this life essence is neces sary to matter, or the physical structure of man. I see oxygen and hydrogen when I look at the manifestation we call ice. When I see water, I know just how oxygen and hydrogen appear when united. So when I look at any form of so-called matter, I know exactly how God appears at that particular time and place. I do not see the effect or works of God, bu I see *God,* and just as much of God, face to face, as I am ca-pable of seeing or recognizing at a certain time.

Step by step, the scientific investigator is being led to the threshold of the awful, absolute Truth, that all matter, or substance, or energy or force-call it what you may is not only intelligent, but is *Pure Intelligence* itself. Atoms, molecules, electrons are but expressions of rates of mo-tion of pure Mind, Thought, or Intelligence that man has personified and called God. Ice is not permeated with water, or controlled by wa-ter. Ice *is* water. Matter is not controlled by mind; mind and matter are *one.* A high vibration of mind does control, to a certain extent, a lower vibration of mind, as water, may carry a lump of ice here or there, water being a more positive rate of activity of the same thing. The particles, so-called, of matter know what to do. The atoms that compose a leaf know when to cohere and materialize a leaf, and they know how and when to disintegrate and dematerialize it: "Thou shalt have no other gods."

I hold in my hand that particular form of the one thing called a rose. Material thought says it is made by God, or that God is in the rose or back of it, or that God caused or created it; but when Spirit, the I Am, asks where is the God that created the rose, where has he

betaken Himself, material belief is silent. But hold a moment I I have here a bud, a half-formed rose. If God makes a rose, He must continue the work to com pletion. Ah, speak softly I Look closely! The rose is now being made, and you say God is making it. Yes, you said God made this full-blown rose. Well, then, He is surely now at work on this half-blown rose. Bring on your spectroscope, your miscroscope I Quick, now, you chemist I Bring on your test-tubes, your acids and alkalis, your spectroscope and X-ray. Analyze, illuminate and magnify! Now we shall discover God. He is here at work before our eyes.

What do you see, chemist? What do you see, scientist? Ah I I know what you see. My experience in the realm of matter and of Spirit tell me what you see. 0 thou stupendous sex force-sex-days of creation, thou Father Mother Yahveh, thou divine male and female, thou eter nal positive and negative dynamis I We now behold thee operating. Out from the chemicalizing mass of God's creative compounds, out of the quivering, vibrating sub stance, slowly comes forth the rose. But are you sure it is a rose? Hold a moment. What is a rose? Of what material is it formed? Ah I the chemist speaks-he of the crucibles and test-tubes and acids I Hear the chemist I

He says, "The rose is made from the universal sub stance," or "The rose is universal substance, in a certain rate of activity." Thanks I Blessed be the chemist! Universal-one verse-one substance-no other substance

-God is the rose, or the smile we call a rose-God is again manifested in the great Eternal IT, for which there is no other name.

Job did not say, "I see the thoughts of God," nor did he say, "I can fathom the mind of God." The plan can not be seen; but that which is planned-a planet-can be seen. One may see the substance of God without under standing the mind of God.

Let us hear Emerson on this stupendous, glorious theme:

"The grJat idea baffies wit; Language falters under it;

It leaves the learned in the lurch- • Nor art, nor power, nor toil can find The measure of the Eternal Mind, Nor hymn, nor prayer, nor church."

0 thou ever-present Divine Mind and Substance I   We now fully realize our oneness with thee, and bathe and revel in thy glory. The mighty Angel of Reality has torn the veil of illusion, and we see the celestial City of Truth with wide-ope gates and the white light of Eternal Love forever upon its streets.

0 thou, in the shadow of sickness and trial, "Take up thy bed and walk; thy sins be forgiven thee."

9

SARA AND ABRAM

S arah or Saria) (Abraham)

WHY was the letter "H" added to Sara and Abram? Heth (cheth) is the 8th letter of the Hebrew alphabet, and means "a field," something per
ceived, or that can be cultivated-in short, spiritual per ception.

In the story of Sarah and Abraham we find the marvel ous truth that age imposes no limit or barrier to the birth of the "Incorruptible Seed" (Peter) for it is *eternal life.*

Sara, at the age of ninety, is told by an angel that she will give birth *to* a child. Abram, at the age of one hun dred, received information that he would be the father of an offspring.

Immediately following these revelations, the letter "H" was added *to* both names. See 16th and 17th chap ters of Genesis.

Abraham and Sarah now find Isaac, which in Hebrew means laugh-ter or happiness.

"Thy seed shall be as the sands of the sea."

"Unto Abraham and hi seed was the promise given; and unto *thy seed,* which is *Christ."-Paul.*

Abraham, Isaac, Jacob, Noah, David, Solomon, Isaiah, etc., etc., are not historical characters. Pontius Pilate, Darius, Pharaoh, Herod, are names of ruling offices, or functions, not certain individuals, no dates being given *to any* so-called transaction in the Scriptures, or to *any* of Paul's Epistles, nor *to* the Acts of the Apostles.

Pilate means "Dart; javelin; a giving up; death." Pontius means "Sea; the open sea." "Marine." He-rod means "Heroic."

Pharaoh, "Rulership."

Darius, "Coercer, conservator" (see presidency, judge ship, etc.).

10

THE WORD OF GOD

, IN the beginning was the word, and the word was with God, and the word was God."-John, 1st Chapter.

"W. 0. R. D." This combination of letters does not mean, in its first and original sense, voice, sound or speech. Physiologically speaking, it means a precious substance.

Therefore, as mankind must be "placed on their feet" physically before the same condition can exist mentally and spiritually, we must get down to fundamentals, and give the physiological meaning of W. 0. R. D.

The Hebrew alphabet consists of 22 letters, each letter having a concrete meaning. In the formation of Hebrew characters, letters were chosen, which, when combined, indicated plainly every phase of that idea which they wished to express.

Let us now take W. 0. R. D., dissect it, and understand the meaning of each letter.

There is no letter "W" in the Hebrew alphabet. That which they used to designate our letter "W" was VV (double V), which is also used in our modern French. Its meaning is "hook." The arm and legs are the hooks of the body.

VV, then, or double V, is the 18th letter of the Hebrew alphabet, and the characters which they used to express that letter, were written thus: TZADDI, almost unpro nouncable. This letter is also, as we write it, the eight eenth in our alphabet. Its number has a great significance. As the ninth letter of the Hebrew alphabet, "Teth," rep resents the equilibrium of the father and mother-the perfcet balance of the male and female, or positive and negative forces, as manifested in the perfected or com pleted human being, so the eighteenth letter, Tzaddi, or double V (VV), is the representation of the fall of spirit toward the material world-or the material body and its

P assions. In astronomy it corresponds with the zodiacal sign, Aquarius.

As the sixth letter of the alphabet, Va *v*, expresses the struggle between the passions and conscience, the antagon ism of ideas, so the eighteenth letter, VV, which is three times six or 666, represents the "beast" which we read of in Revelation, the Adam man. On the mental plane we use the expression He Phren, for this number, the lower mind, the material mind. In astronomy the affinity of this letter (6) is the bull (Taurus). Mankind, living *wholly* on the material plane, is hence a beast-a beast physically, mentally and emotionally. Animal on three planes. Thus in the Tarot we find that 18 represents "Antagonism."

Placing the two V's togther, one over the other, they represent the two arms and the two legs of the unregen erated man, as the upper V or triangle points *downward*. In the regenerated man the hands are folded together over the head in adoration of divinity, and thus the apex points upward. In the lower triangle the same change takes place, the forces hitherto misused, going *downward* and *outward* are sent upward and returned to the "Holy of Holies," the triangle becomes closed at the bottom and opened upward.

The letter "W," then, or VV, represents the earthly or Adam man, the material body and the lower mind.

The letter "O," the sixteenth letter of the alphabet, written Ayin,·in Hebrew, has somewhat the same mean ing as the first letter, but in a deeper sense alludes to a material *building,* an operation in the visible and material world. "The *materialization* of God, the Holy Spirit, the entrance of the Holy Spirit into the visible world," the Tarot tells us.

Since God, One, is individual or undivided and undifferentiated, to manifest in the material plane, God or THAT must *divide,* must become two halves of the circle, must manifest as positive and negative, male and female, electricity and magnetism. From this we deduce the expression, "dual power" or "dual operation"

-"dual force." In astronomy this is represented by the sign Capricorn. These dual forces, operating within us,

t hus become the Goat, which "Bears away the sins of the world" (circle-material body).

In the average human being, this dual power is not operating in_harmony. The action is unequal. If these two currents operated in harmony in the human body, the regenerated man would be manifested, the *flesh* would have become the WORD itself.

The letter "R" is the twentieth letter, written "Resh," and the symbolism of this letter is most wonderful. It represents the head of man and is, therefore, associated with the idea/of original and determined *movement.* It is the sign of *motion* itself, good, or bad, and expresses the renewal of things with regard to their innate power of motion. It corresponds to Saturn. "Resh" also sym bols rest. A ship may rest on water that is in motion.

The description of the inner meaning of this letter, in the Tarot, throws a flood of light upon it as used in its present position in W.O.R.D., as it has a deep esoteric significance. To quote: "A tomb opens in the earth, and a man, woman and child issue from it; their hands are joined in sign of adoration. How can the reawakening of nature *under the influence of the WORD,* be better expressed? We must admire the way in which the sym bol answers to the corresponding Hebrew hieroglyphic."

Comment on the above quotation is scarcely necessary, yet for the convenience of those not yet able to figure it out for themselves, let it be said, that the tomb, cave or manger, is the *birth place* of the seed, the **WORD,** the "Son of man" which redeems the Adam man, *IF NOT IN-*

TERFERED WITH. *"Under the influence of the Word,"* indeed, is the carnal man, "dead in trespass and sin," reborn to a new life.

The letter "D," the fourth in the Hebrew alphabet, as also in ours, is written "Daleth," and means the womb, or door, mouth. It denotes abundance springing from di vision. "Thus Daleth expresses a creation made by a being according to *divine* laws. It expresses domination of spirit over matter. The Tarot thus wonderfully inter prets its meaning: "In the Divine, Reflex of the Father, it is the will. In the Human, Reflex of Adam, it is power.

God-Man: The Word Made Flesh

In the Natural, Reflex of Natura naturans, it is the uni versal creative fluid, the soul of the Universe. In astron omy its affinity is Jupiter."

Summing this up we can see that the letter "D" stands for the solar plexus in the human body, as it is the *reflec tion* of the true sun (the Father), and the source of all things.

W.O.R.D., then, means this: The creation, according to *divine laws, from the universal creative fluid,* in the tomb, cave or manger of the earth (solar plexus), of that PERFECT ONE (SEED, fish, fruit, Jesus) Vishnu, Joshua, Moses, Horus, etc., etc., which has the power to spir- itualize-regenerate the Adam man, so that he be comes the "Lord God from heaven"-the WORD MADE FLESH." "And the Word was made *flesh* and dwelt among us."-John 1:14.

We realize, then, that word does not refer to speech. The Hebrew let- ter which signifies speech is Phe, the seventeenth letter. It refers to the force which dispenses the essence of life, which gives it the means of per- petually renewing its creations after destruction. We can speak destruc- tively and we have the power to speak construc tively.

The two letters "O" and "R" combined are used to specify a precious substance, originally ref erred to as "gold," for the ancients realized that the sun's rays, which they called "golden," precipitated in the human body and formed creative substance.

The Bible"tells us that "Man does not live by bread alone, but by every word (or seed) , that proceedeth out of the mouth of God," proving that, in order to truly live, we must save the precious substance. In anatomy, the passage way undernearth the sutures which leads down into the thalamus, is the mouth of God, for it is from the cerebrum, the upper brain, that the most wonderful "gift" to the human body comes. This represents the unseen "mouth." The visible mouth is the solar plexus.

We can turn to the pages of Gray's Anatomy, or any good medical dictionary, and examine carefully the illus tration of a 26-day old foetus. We see, then, that almost

t he entire body c'onsists of brain substance-in fact, it looks like an elongated brain. The upper brain, or Father-Mother substance, is what furnishes the material from which the body is made. Verily it is the Aloha, the beginning. Degenerates, and· people living in excesses, have become greatly deficient in this precious material, and the whole appearance of the body testifies to the dese cration of the temple.

Man can become regenerated, and thus save his soul, which is sown in corruption, so that it may be raised in corruption.
/   ,

We can compare speech with the operations of the processes of the planets. "The heavens declare the glory of God, and the firmament showeth his handiwork.

"Day unto day u_ttereth speech, and night unto night showeth knowledge. •

"There is no *speech* or *language* where their voice is not heard."

The heavens, or the planets in the heavens, have their own particular influence, operation or speech, upon this planet of ours. We admit that the moon rules the tides, that without the sun we could not live, so why deny the influence of the other planets.

Thus we see, from the foregoing, that word, and voice or speech are two entirely different things, and that John meant the precious creative substance when he spoke of the "WORD."

"Now this is the parable. The *SEED* IS THE *WORD* OF GOD."-Luke 8:11.

"Seed, word" and "God," are all synonyms of one and the same thing-the· wonderful creative substance, the universal esse, from which all things are brought forth, and in which all things are. The Scriptures, or allegories and parables of the Bible, are the only writings that give us information as to what the Word of God is. There fore, in this book, we will quote what is written there in regard to it.

Seed is the cause, the nucleus of everything, therefore a seed is "the *beginning.*" In the beginning was the WORD."

The fluid, oil, or marrow which flows down the spinal cord, comes from the upper brain, the Creator or Father, the "Most High," and is known in physiology as ovum, or generative seed-that life essence which creates the human form of corruptible flesh. In the Greek, from which the New Testament was translated, this marrow is called Christ, which is the Greek word for oil.

When this oil is refined, transmuted, lifted up, raised, it becomes so highly vitalized that it regenerates the body and "overcomes" the last *enemy,* death.

How can it be lifted up?

By lifting up the "Son of man," the seed, the word, the savior. The oil (Christ) in the spinal cord, is the salt which is mentioned in the Bible, and the savior is the seed, or Jesus.

The salt and the savior both come from the same source-the same place-the Father-the upper brain. In the Bible allegory the seed, Jesus, is made to say, "Without my Father I can do nothing." The material from the Father which forms the seed, has gone through a different process from that which forms the oil. The chemical formula of the oil is J.O.H.N., and Jesus was baptized or anointed *of* John, not *by* John, as it is incor rectly quoted. (See article on **OIL).**

If we lift up or raise the oil in the spinal cord, by the power of the seed, by saving it, it must be a physiological and chemical operation within the body of each of us.

Such is the·case.

There is no mystery, no marvel in all the universe that is greater than man himself. "Man know thyself" con fronts us, down through the ages, but only a few have paid attention to the voice of the Delphic oracle- only a few have looked within.

There is a wonderful "Strait and narrow way," a *real strait, not straight,* which extends from the upper brain, the cerebrum, to the end of the spinal cord, otherwise named Jordan, in the Bible. We find that the meaning of this in Hebrew is, descender or "River of God." The "Strait and narrow way is, indeed, the River of God, for it leads to the Father-the Most High-the upper brain.

As the Jordan edipties into the Dead Sea, so the spinal cord termi- nates in that section of the anatomy, which is designated, in the medical terminolgy as *Sodom.* Josephus refers to the region as the "Lake of Sodom," and in other writings we find it referred to as the "Sea of Lot," and "Lake Asphaltus."

The student of symbology can easily see thztt it is the slimy pool from which springs up the lotus, whose flower of a thousand petals blooms forth, reflecting in its golden heart the image of its creator.

The wondlrful pneumogastric nerve, rising in the floor or the fourth ventricle of the head, and connected with the cerebellum, crosses the spinal cord, or Jordan, at the base of the Skull Golgotha, and sends nu- merous branches to throat, lungs, heai;t and stomach, terminating in a plexus under the latter organ, which is named the androgynous brain, the stomach brain, or solar plexus. This wonderful nerve has six differ- ent physical functions, in addition to the deeply esoteric office of being the channel for the Holy Breath, or Holy Ghost, without which there would be no conception of the Holy Child, the WORD.

In Bible terminology the solar plexus also means man ger, cave, Bethlehem, for it is in the centre of this plexus of nerves that we find the thimble-shaped cavity or de pression from which issues forth the redeemer of the Adam man. In a dual sense it is the "house of bread," as it is the place where the divine bread or seed is formed, and it lies directly back of the house of material bread, the stomach. "Man shall not live by bread alone, but by every WORD (seed) that cometh from the mouth of God." Jesus was born in Bethlehem, and this word means in Hebrew "house (Beth) of bread (lehem)." See how wonderfully the Hebrew words expressed the true mean ing of the hidden truth. "I am the bread of life."

In the central part of the head is the wonderful cham ber or bed, called the "thalamus." Santee's Anatomy of the Brain and Spinal Cord" describes it thus: "It is the great ganglion of the inter-brain. The thalamus is an important sensory relay station. Its medial part is con cerned with smell and its lateral part with common sensa-

t ion and taste. According to Head and Holmes, it is also an organ of consciousness for impulses of pain and temperature. The third ventricle separates the thalami from each other, except at the mid-point where they are joined by the MASSA INTERMEDIA. The thalamus is situated behind and medial to the corpus striatum, and projects backward over the mid-brain. Laterally it rests against the superior lamina·of the internal capsule, which separated it from the lentiform nucleus. The thalamus is shaped like an egg, with the small end directed forward.

It measures 4 cm. or about one and one-half inches in length and 2.5 cm. of one inch in width and thickness. It has an interior and posterior extremity and four surfaces; superior, inferior, medial and lateral."

The most striking statement in the above paragraph is, that the thalamus is egg-shaped, and we can readily see why there is so much reference made, in ancient religions, to the egg. For the thalamus with its adjacent append ages, when viewed in cross sections of the brain, looks ex actly like a beetle, the body egg shaped, and the "horns" of the lateral ventri-cle, typifying the horns of the beetle. In the scarabaeus of Egypt is exem-plified the egg of im mortality, the light of the world. It is the chamber, the HOLY OF HOLIES, wherein is concealed the ark of the covenant. In the Egyptian Book of the Dead we find this referred to as the "Boat of Seker." Every religion, which has existed down through the ages, has told in its own terminology, the same story, the same physiological process taking place within the body of man.

On the posterior side of the thalamus we find the pineal body. It is a cone-shaped body, 6 mm *(0.25* in.) high and 4 mm (0.17 in.) in diame-ter, joined to the roof of the third ventricle by a flattened stalk, the habe-nula. Santee tells us that "The interior of the pineal body is made up of closed follicles surrounded by ingrowths of connective tissue. The fol-licles are filled with epithelial cells mixed with *calcareous* (lime) matter, the *brain-sand* (acerculus cerebri). Calcareous deposits are found also
on the pineal stalk and along the choi-ioid plexuses,.   The
function of the pineal body is unknown.   Des Cartes

facetiously suggesis that it is the abode of the spirit (the
sand of man."

The most significant statement in the above paragraph, to the eso-teric student, is the reference to the calcareous deposit-the brain-sand. Now, indeed, do we find the words of the great occultist, Madame He-lena Pretrovna Blavatsky, written nearly half a century ago, justified, proved true in the light of modern science. Who now dares to lightly cast aside the statements of seers and mystics recorded in secret and sa-cred doctrines, as unre liable and untrue?

The upper section of this pineal body is the optic, or eye, the "All-seeing Eye," it is the wonderful light of the candle, which "Gives light to the whole house."

This pineal body is the *male spiritual organ.* If you ask for proof as to"its being a male organ, you can find indubitable proof by referring to any good physiological chart or anatomy, for you will see that the lower portions of this organ has been given the names, "corpora quad rigemina," which means "four-fold bodies"-two nates (buttocks), and two testes (testicles). Thus we see, that in spite of our incredulence, even the scoffing scientist has unwittingly demonstrated the truth of occult investiga tions, in respect to this body.

In esoteric as well as physiological meaning, this is Joseph, meaning to increase, the father of Jesus, the seed, the redeemer. It is the organ through which the electrical forces of the body play. It is, in other words, *one* of the *differentiators* of *THAT-the* universal esse deposited, materialized, in the cerebrum, the upper brain. In the Medieval Hebrew, as quoted from the Sacred Books of the East, it is referred to as "The Crystalline Dew" from heaven, deposited in the cranium. The marvelous sym bology of our own Bible is duplicated in *all* the ancient Scriptures, in all the nations of the world. Some of this wonderful esse, this Father, flows down from the upper brain into the pineal body, where it is differentiated becomes masculine, positive, electrical, in quality and action.

On the other side of the thalamus is located the pituit

a ry body, the *feminine spiritual organ.* It is a small, reddish, ellipsoid organ in a depression of the sphenoid bone, and is attached to the brain by a peduncle. It has two lobes, one of yellowish-gray and the other reddish gray color. It secretes a mucous or phlegm, and the latter substance is what gives it its name. It also receives its secretion from the Father, the universal ESSE, the undifferentiated substance from which all things are brought forth. Flowing into this gland it becomes mag netic, female, in its quality and action. It is the Mare, Mary, pure sea or water, the Mother of the Holy Child. The pine.al gland is directly referred to in the Bible as Mount Penial, where Jacob wrestled with the Angel of the Lord. In Hebrew the word means "Face of God." It is indeed the face of God. The top of this gland being the eye. Where can the eye be located save in the face?

Connected with the pinal gland is a nerve called the "pingala" in secret writings. This nerve crosses the spinal cord at the base of the skull, in the medulla oblongata, and follows down the right side of the spinal cord to its end.

Likewise, connected with the pituitary body, is the nerve Ida, which crosses the spinal cord at the same place where the Pingala crosses, follows down the left side of the spinal cord to its base. Here the two nerves converge into the body through the semi-luna ganglion, where they merge into the solar plexus.

The divine esse which has been differentiated by enter ing these two glands has become Mary and Joseph, the mother and father of the holy child. This material, this actual substance, enters the solar plexus where it combines with the Holy Breath and the seed is born the bread is made which is intended to be eaten in the "Father's Kingdom."

The first seed is formed in the solar plexus of every individual, commencing at the age of twelve, which we have designated as the age of puberty. Thereafter, it is

formed every 29.½ days, this taking place in each indi

vidual at the time of the month when the moon is in the sign in which the sun was at the birth of the individual.

Herod, Pharabh, the passions, desires and emotions, seek to slay this Divine Babe.

Here we will quote the Sanscrit statement in regard to the danger always present for the seed, child, fruit or *fish,* as given in Vol. II of the Secret Doctrine, by H. P. Blavatsky:

"While Vaivasvata was engaged in devotion on the river bank, a FISH craves his protection from a bigger FISH. He *saves* it and places it in a jar (solar plexus) which, growing larger and larger, communicates to him the news of t;he forthcoming deluge. (Nate gold fish in jar).

"Vaivasvata Manu, the *Son of Surya, the Sun,* and the *Savior* of our race, *is connected with the seed of life, both* physically and spiritually."

The significance o,f the above is apparent.

In the Bible we find this statement: "Joseph shall have a double portion."

Joseph was one of the children of Jacob, which means "circle" in Hebrew. His name was afterwards changed to Israel, so that the sons of Jacob are also the sons of Israel. The signs of the Zodiac are also referred to as the children of Jacob, and when applied in physiology, refer to the solar plexus, and the twelve forces centered there. All the forces which enter the body of man are received in this part of the body, and are sent out from there. Joseph represents one of these divisions or centers, and this is one of his portions. The other is the pineal gland, that also being Joseph.

Thus all the so-called tribes referred to as Gad, Rheu ben, Levi, etc., etc., refer to the forces operative in the human body, and not to bodies of people.

We find, then, this seed, fruit, fish, bread and savior, born in the solar plexus.

We must lift up, save, or raise this seed. "If I be lifted up I will draw all men unto me."-John 12 :32.

It must be taken into the spinal cord or, in other words, be baptized of JOHN. It must be anointed with oil.

We find that there is oil present in the spinal cord. This subject will be dealt with elsewhere in this book.

In the book of Joshua, we find the story of the Ark of the MOST HIGH GOD being taken by the Priests of the Twelve Tribes into the Jordan, and again, in the New Testament we find the identical story in the baptism of Jesus of John (oil), in the Jordan. The Hebrews told their story, in the Old Testament, and the Greeks gave theirs in the New Testament.

In Joshua's (fish in Hebrew) story we find that he commanded the sun and moon to stand still, while he slew his enemies. The semi-lunar ganglion, which is attached to the solar plexus, is identical with the moon. Nerves from this plexus extend to the lower parts of the body and, in fact, connect with the organs of generation. No wonder Joshua commanded these forces to be still so that the seed could pass into the Jordan in safety. For, we find that just below this passageway into the spinal cord is another, called the "fish-gate," which leads directly to the genitals. If the lower desires are not stilled this seed or fish will be "swallowed," killed by the generative fish.

When these lower forces are controlled, the High Priests of the body, the higher forces, are in command, and the seed is taken into the Jordan.

"At the time of the flood, when the Jordan overflowed its banks" and "stood up," was the Ark carried into the Jordan. This proves conclusively the exact location, physiologically, of the entrance into the spinal cord. For this portion of the cord is the broadest-it is where it "stands up," or contacts with that part of the anatomy termed Sodom and Gomorrah.

At the place where the **ARK** entered the "water," twelve men were chosen to set up stones, and the Bible tells us that "They are there to *this day."* These twelve stones correspond to the twelve Dorsal vertebrae, to each vertebra of which a nerve is attached that forms part of the solar plexus. These twelve nerves terminate in the solar plexus. They are the twelve priests whose serv ices enabled the Ark to enter the "River of God."

The twelve forces, then, bore this ARK *up* out of the water.

I They broke down the walls of Jericho and entered the city with the ARK of the MOST HIGH GOD.

In the New Testament story Jesus was baptized in the Jordan. Then, when the time came for His crucifixion, He went *to* the Garden of Gethsemene. In anatomy this is near the Medulla Oblongata, with the olives on either

side, a physiological *fact,* as any anatomy proves. There are two "pyramids," also, at this place.

In anatomy, Golgotha (place of the skull, in Hebrew) is the base of the skull, where the spinal cord enters the head. At this point is a double cross made by the Adi, the Pingala and the pneumogastric nerves. They are the St. George and St. Andrew crosses, with the form of a man displayed therein. Many very ancient Byzantine coins and frescoes show this deeply esoteric symbol. This same eight-pointed··star or combined crosses appears on amulets and seals of ancient Chaldea, Babylon, Assyria, Persia and India.

Can we any longer doubt that the ancient records told the same story as is found in our own Scriptures, and that it was all in regard to one thing, one process, the MAS TERY OF THE BODY?

The seed, then, is crucified on the cross, it is raised in power, for nowhere does the crucifixion mean *death*.

We "cross" animals to improve the breed, the qualities. Crossed electric wires produce a more powerful current. By the process of crossing, or crucifixion, therefore, this seed took on added power, in fact, recetved the "illumina tion," which the seed had previously *asked* for "The hour has come. Father, glorify thy Son that thy Son may glorify thee."

At the moment of glorification or illumination, the seed *did not* say "My God, my God, why hast thou forsaken me." It is a gross mistranslation. It, moreover, is not at all in keeping with the tenor of the request, just prev ious to passing onto the cross. The correct translation of this exclamation, is "My God, my God, how thou dost glorify me." Does not this seem more in keeping with the calm and earnest request "Father, the hour has come, glorify thy Son that thy Son may glorify thee?"

Read John and note glory and glorify. John, or Ioannes, is ointment, or oil, here personified.

Glorify means to illuminate-to give light-glow ray. The passing of the seed over the crossed nerves, and its passage into the pineal gland does, in very truth, cause the illumination-the flash of light, the raising or illumi nation of consciousness of the individual in which this process is *allowed* to take place. For it is man that pre- vents its accomplishment. .

After the crucifixion the "body" of Jesus is claimed by Joseph, and it is taken by him into his own tomb, where no man had ever been laid. This Joseph is the same Joseph-the father of Jesus, the pineal gland, for no other man, no seed had been absorbed by the gland prev iously, for this is the first seed that has been saved. In other words, the Son returns to the Father, the seed re turns to its source. The Father and the Son have become ONE.

No other explanation save a physiological one can make clear this statement of Jesus. "And greater things than I do, ye shall do, for I go unto my Father." The first seed that has been saved apparently makes this statement. When the first seed is saved, the entire body is changed. It vibrates at a higher rate, the fluids are purer. In 29_½ days another seed is born, and the material from which this seed is formed is of a more refined *substance*, of greater power. Therefore, when it is crucified, is it not of greater power than the first seed? The third seed will also have been raised to the third power, and so on. The entire body is chanl!ed by the raising or saving of each seed. Paul says, "Ye are *transformed* by the renewing of your minds." The mind, the brain, is indeed renewed by each seed that is carried into the pineal gland, with the accompanying oil. "And the ransomed of the Lord shall return and come to Zion, with songs and everlasting joy."

This, then, is the process whereby the WORD, which is also GOD AND SEED, regenerated, transforms the Adam man, so that he becomes the "LORD GOD from heaven."

There are mariy direct references to the process, among which are the following:

Corinthians 11 :28, "_But let a man examine himself and
so eat of that bread and drink of that cup."

11:29, "For he that eateth and drinketh unworthily, eateth and drinketh damnation to himself, not discerning the *Lord's body.*" Damn or damnation simply means to check or stop the "going on" or procedure.

Cor. **11** :30, "For this cause many are weak and sickly among you, and many sleep."

Acts I, "Ye men of Galilee, why stand ye gazing up into heaven? This same Jesus, which is *taken up from you,* into heaven, shall so come in *like manner* as ye have seen him go into heaven."

II John, 7th verse, "He that confesseth not that Jesus Christ *is* come in the flesh, the same is Anti-Christ."

John 3 :3, "Jesus answered and said unto him, verily, verily I say unto thee, except a man be born again, he cannot see the kingdom of heaven."

1st John 3 :9, "Whosoever is born of God *doth not* commit sin, for his *seed* remaineth *in him,* and he cannot sin because he is born of God."

Peter 1 :23, "Being born again, not of corruptible *seed,* but of incorruptible, by the WORD OF GOD, which liveth and abideth forever."

Luke 4 :4, "And Jesus answered him, saying, it is writ ten that man shall not *live* by bread alone, but by every WORD of God."

Galatians 3 :16, "Now to Abraham and his seed were these promises made, and to *thy seed* which is *Christ."*

Luke 8: 11, "Now the parable is this; the *seed is the WORD OF GOD."*

Colossians 1 :26-27, "Even the mystery which hath been hid from ages and generations, but now is made manifest to his saints. To whom God would make known what is the riches of the glory of this mystery among the Gentiles, which is CHRIST IN YOU, THE HOPE OF GLORY."

Deut. 28 :38, "Thou shalt carry much seed out into the

field, and thou shalt *gather but little in;* for the locust shall consume it." Eating, devouring or gluttony. (See John the Baptist.)

Matthew 13 :27, "He answered and said unto them. He that soweth the good seed is the Son of man." (The Seed is the Son of Man.)

II Cor. 9 :10, "Now he that ministereth seed to the sower doth minister bread for your food, and multiply your seed sown, and increase the fruits of your righteous ness."

John 6 :58, "This is that bread which came down from heaven; not as your fathers did eat manna and are dead. He that eateth of this bread shall LIVE FOREVER." John 6:51, "I am the LIVING BREAD WHICH

CAME DOWN FROM HEAVEN. If any man eat of this bread he shall live forever; and the bread that I will give is my flesh, which I will give for the life of the world."   •

1st Cor. 15 :21, "For since by man came death, by man came also the resurrection of the dead."

Isaiah 45 :23, "The word is gone out of my mouth." Matthew 34:25, "My word shall not pass away."

John 17 :8, "I have given them the word thou gavest me."

Psalms 119 :130, "The *entrance of thy word* giveth
light."

The phrase, "The truth in a nut shell," has a deep occult mean-ing.   "I am the truth."

"My WORD shall not return unto me void, but it shall accomplish that whereunto it was sent."

Acts 13 :26, "To you is the WORD of salvation sent."

Hebrews 2 :2, "The WORD of God is quick and powerful."

Hebrews 6 :5, "Have tasted the good WORD of God."

Peter 2 :2, "The sincere milk of the WORD."

Isaiah 30 :23, "Thou shalt be given the rain of thy seed, that thou shalt sow the ground withal; and bread of the increase of the earth and it shall be fat and plenteous."

Psalms 68 :11, "The Lord gave the WORD."

And yet Smitli's Bible Dictionary, in its seeming efforts to find the meaning of "WORD," fails to quote Luke 8 :11 *"The SEED IS THE WORD OF GOD."* Why

is it? Was it because the immortal statement *proves* beyond peradven-ture that the seed within us is the *savior* and not a *man without?* Error dies hard, but it *always* dies, and "Amid its worshippers."

..;& ..;& ..;&

WHAT WAS THE "WORD OF THE LORD" THAT CAME SO OFTEN TO THE

OLD-TIME PROPHETS?

,.., "The Seed is the *word"-Luke 8:11.*

In all the statements in the Bible that refer to the "Word of the Lord," we find the same great truth told over and over again in the Hebrew Scriptures and trans lated "Word of the Lord"-the *Seed.*

"And the word of the Lord came to Jeremiah," or "Joel" or "Ezekiel" or "Hosea."

And thus it followed that after each seed had been saved, the Prophet foretold, admonished and preached truth to the world.

TRANSMUTATION-TURNING WATER INTO WINE

THE Lord of transmutation has ascended the throne of Aquarius to rule the world for 2160 years.

Aquarius, the fifth Son, Sun, of Jacob, circle, or to follow after, is Dan, Hebrew for Judge. Thus the day or time of judgment or understanding will have for its executor the revolutionary planet Uranus, or as it is in Greek, "Oranous." Uranus virtually means *Son of Heaven.*

This God is surely a suitable ruler for the zodiacal Sign Aquarius, the *Man.* "And then shall appear the *Sign* of the Son (Sun) of man in the heavens.'

The solar system now being in Aquarius we may expect, and as a matter of fact are experiencing, the prophecies of great astrologians as recorded in Matt. 24th, also Luke 21st.

In the Judgment Day, or time of knowledge, we are due to realize the process by which base metals are trans muted into gold.

The word gold comes from Or, a product of the Sun's rays or the breath of life.

Life or Spirit breathed into man precipitates brain cells and gray matter which create or build the fluids and structure of physical man.

Or is the seed or W *or* d-L *or* d, etc.

"In the beginning was the word * * * the *word*
was God."

God means power.

Thus the emanations from Sun, basic material, are changed to gold, and the process eternally proceeding is being recognized by man at the present day, due to the fact that the planet of gold, Oranous, is now ruling Earth and thereby bringing good judgment upon the people.

Both in Greek and Hebrew any fluid, air, or ether was called water until organized; then it was wine. The rain that falls on the ground and taken up into the organism of !r7e, vegetable or fruit is changed into wine, *i. e.,* sap

or Jutce.

The parable of turning water into wine at the marriage at Cana in Galilee is a literal statement of a process taking place with every heart beat in the human organism.

Galilee means a circle of water or fluid-the circulatory system. Cana means a dividing place, the lungs or reeds, the tissue and, cells of the lungs.

Biochemists have shown that food does not form the organic part of blood, but simply furnishes the mineral base by setting free the inorganic or cell-salts contained in all foodstuff. The organic part, oil, fibrin, albumen, etc., contained in food is, burned or digested in the stomach and intestinal tract, to furnish motive power to operate the human machine and draw air into lungs, Cana, thence into arteries, *i. e.,* air carriers. Therefore, it is clearly shown that air (spirit) unites with the minerals and forms blood, proving that the oil, albumen, etc., found in blood, is created every breath at the "marriage of Cana of Galilee."

Air was called water or the pure sea; viz.: Virgin

Mar-y. So we see how water is changed into wine-blood

-every moment.

In the new age, we will need perfect bodies to corre spond with the higher vibration, or motion of the new blood, for "old bottles (bodies), cannot contain the new wine."

Another allegorical statement, typifying the same truth reads, "And I saw a new Heaven and a New Earth,"i. *e.,* new mind and new body.

Biochemistry may well say with Walt Whitman, "To the sick lying on their backs I bring help, and to the strong, upright man I bring more needed help." To be grouchy, cross, irritable, despondent, or easily discour aged, is prima facie evidence that the fluids of the stomach, liver, and brain are not vibrating at normal rate, the rate that results in equilibrium or health. Health cannot be qualified, *i. e.,* poor health or good health. There must

be either health or dishealth; ease or disease. We do not say poor ease or good ease. We say ease or dis-ease, viz., not at ease.

A sufficient amount of the cell-salts of the body properly combined taken as food-'-not simply to cure some ache, pain or exudation-forms blood that materializes in healthy fluids, flesh and bone tissue.

We should take the tissue cell-salts as one uses health foods, not simply to change health to health, but to keep the rate of blood vibration in the tone of health all the time.

Biochemistry is'the sign-board pointing to the open country, to hills and green fields of health and the truth that shall set the seeking Ego free from poverty and disease.

Conservation and transmutation obtain in all the com mercial world. The force of falling water is transmuted into the product of the factories. Steam, the vibration of copper and carbon discs that turn night into day, the automobiles, "chariots that run like lightning and jostle each other in the streets," are the effects of the transmu tation of base or basic material.

On some fair tomorrow when the subtle vibrations of the Aquarian Age, directed by Oranous, shall have awak ened and called to action the millions of dormant cells of the wondrous brain, man will by the power of the *lost word* restored, conserve and transmute the mineral sub stance of his body, the soul, IO H N, and with the "product" the precious oint-ment-ail, *Christ,* triumph over the cross at Golgotha and ascend to the pineal gland that transmits the christed Son to the Optic Thalamus, the all-seeing Eye of the chamber, and thus furnish "light to all that are in the house."

In these latter days our business world has been domi

nated by a great oil trust, petroleum, mineral oil, petra stone, rock or mineral and oleum; oil was exploited, and then by the law of transmutation changed into gasoline. The transmutation of gasoline by the miracle of the "conservation of energy" causes the *"ascension"* of the air ship, and the pathway of the Eagle and the open road

of man lie parallel across the vaulted sky.

And when the Ego shall have triumphed over the car nal mind and transmuted the crude soul fluids into the gold of the "New Wine," it will ascend to the Father, the upper brain.

"And the temple needs no light of the Sun by day nor Moon by night, for the light of the Lard doth lighten it." The gospel miracle of turning water into wine is found only in John and appears as a companion piece to the multiplication of the loaves .and fishes. The meaning of miracle is: "To uncover a truth."

We are indebted to Lawrence Parmly Brown for much of the followi g: (See open Court, May, 1920.)

"This beginning of the signs (or 'miracles') Jesus did in Cana of Galilee, and manifested his glory; and his dis ciples believed on him." This is the first miracle of Jesus, according to John, jqst as the changing of the waters to blood was the first plague inflicted upon the Egyptians as one of the miracles of Moses. But the J ohannine mar riage-feast appears to have been recognized as a variant of the great feast of Rabbinical tradition, which is to in augurate the coming of the Messiah, and at which he shall drink wine made from the grapes that grew in Paradise during the six days of creation and were since preserved in Adam's cave (Buxdorf, *Synod. Jud.,* p. 460). The *Fo-pen-hing-tsi-king,* a Chinese life of Gautama Buddha, relates that this last Buddha declared that when one of his predecessors attended a wedding in the city of Jambunada, he not only kept the foods and drinks miraculously undiminished during the feast, but caused the host's uninvited guests to come and partake of it, even as the host had silently wished (according to Lillie, *Buddhism in Christianity,* pp. 169, 170; *Popular Life of Buddha,* pp. 305, 306).

Compare Eucharistic bread and wine to the flesh and blood of Jesus in the Roman Catholic doctrine.

Words for "bread" are sometimes employed for all solid foods that are transmuted into the flesh or bodies of men, while water or (red) wine is conceived to be changed into blood: Wine is often called the "blood of grapes" or the "blood of the grape," as in the Old Testament (Gen. xlix. 11 ; Deut. xxxii. 14, etc.) ; and the

juice of the grape is naturally conceived as having been transmuted from water by the heat of the sun, which is also the chief factor in the fermentation of wine.

In the Egyptian legend of Horus of Edfu, that god smites the enemies of Ra, and the latter says to the former: " 'Thou makest the water of Edfu (red with blood) like grapes, and thy heart is rejoiced thereat.' Hence the water of Edfu is called (the water of grapes)" (Sayce, *Rel. dnc. Eg. and Bab.,* p. 220). In the Destruction of Mankind, the deluge is poured out from seven thousand jars of human blood, representing the red color of the Nile waters shortly after the beginning of the inundation *(Records of the Past,* VI, pp. 105-112).

The mythic marriage is primarily that of the sun (see Phredrus, I, /ab. 6), either with the earth or the moon whence, doubtless, the Athenians at one time celebrated marriages at the new moon (when she was in conjunction with the sun-Proclus *ad Hesiod. Oper.,* 782). Practically nothing is related of the Johannine bridegroom.

and there is no reference to the bride; but in the mythic view the bridegroom is a mere variant of Jesus (the figurative "bridegroom" of John iii. 29, cf. Mark. ii. 19, 20, etc.), while his mother and the bride are duplications of wider variation. Thus the Virgin Mary is often called the

Rose of Sharon and Lily of Israel; epithets from Can ticles ii, where the bride is "a rose of Sharon and a lily of the valleys," who is brought by the bridegroom to "the banqueting-house"-literally "the house of wine," as in the Septuagint.

12

JOHN THE BAPTIST

J OHN, or Ioannes,. is the ointment, oil, that flows down the spinal cord from the reservoir of God sub stance in the upper brain, the "Most High," the

heaved-up place, the Heave-n, within.   .

"VVe know .that we have in heaven a more enduring

substance."-Paul.

The mysterious circumstances connected with the Bible story of John the Baptist and the information given in Smith's Bible Dictionary prove the wholly divine origin of that which was cal.led "John," but which means oil in Greek. John's father was said to be a priest of Ahia, or Abijah. This latter, in Hebrew, means "Whose father is Jehovah." Jehovah is the upper brain, the Most High

-the "crystalline dew" referred *to* in Medieval Hebrew. Before the oil is raised by the seed, thus giving one

tenth (tithe) to the Lord, it is called "natural" or "wild," "not cultivated," like wild flowers-"wild honey." So John was a wild man-a native. A parable? Most certainly I

"His food was locusts and wild honey."

The pineal gland and the pituitary body secret fluids called milk and honey in the Scriptures.

Locust means destructive, devourer-a glutton.

Deut. 28 :42: "All thy tree (tree of life and fruit seed) shall the locusts (sex desire) consume."

The reader will please remember that the Bible is *Secret* Doctrine, or that which is *within* and not without. History is a record of outward things.

John, the natural man, was an eater of the•fruit of the tree of life, with a *girdle of camel's hair* (from Gimel the 3rd letter of the Hebrew alphabet, which pertains to the external male organ). *But* John, like the prodigal son, changed his mind and is made to say, "One cometh *after me* (to get me) the latchet of whose shoes (pisces-the feet-fishes) I am not worthy to unloose."

Latchet and shoes are mblems of cover, or cup swaddling cloth. The oil in the seed, when born, is cov ered or protected by a crust of mineral salts, which, when anointed by being baptized in Jordan (John), is loosened ("He that saveth his life shall *loosen* it." See mistrans lation of Scripture) in order that the shell may fall apart when the seed, Jesus, goes over the cross, thus, "Father, remove the cup (cover *or* latchet) from me," in order that the precious material may ascend into the pineal gland.

13

THE PLAGUES OF EGYPT

THESE same locusts, sex appetite, gluttony, or de vourers, are and always have been the plagues, *i. e.,* sickness and disease in all peoples in all ages.

And now, when evil doers wax worse and worse, a ma jority of human beings are deliberately and "with malice aforethought," committing suicide, through eating and drinking for *pleasure,* and indulging in sexual excesses on every plane, in every way known to carnal perverts.

Officers of the law tell us that licentiousness has surely reached its limit. The "Hand-writing on the Wall" appears. In proof of this allow us to quote the following by the great poet, Rabindranath Tagore, printed in the August 1st issue of the Los Angeles Examiner: "Paris, July 31.-I came from Asia expecting to find Europe a vale of tears, a desert of misery and grief. With ten million dead-10,000,000 stricken suddenly by shell or bullet from the roster of the earth, snatched from their firesides and their babies and the women whom they loved

-what should one visualize but a Europe draped in black, a Europe where the innocent laughter of a tiny child would seem a gross incongruity?

"Yet Europe weeps not. She has cast off her black, and is wearing her brightest colors, her most splendid plumes. Her men are already forgetting their slaught ered brothers in the incessant effort to profit from the abnormal financial conditions prevailing because of the war; her women-ah, her women I They are snatching flowers, bright red poppies, from the graves of their fallen husbands and sons, to wear them in their hair.

"Ten million dead-and naught but dust already I

Were these 10,000,000 the only sober, sane living people in Europe? Are those who are left only those consumed with avarice, selfishness and the desire to be amused at no matter what cost? Or is this Europe, which is dancing on its own coffin. a Europe gone stark mad?

"Paris, turn thine eyes to the south. There a templed **city** once stood, a living, breathing defiance to an inevitable death-a death that came sooner than it thought, and overwhelmed it. The name of that city was Babylon. Well named was Babylon! Well named also Paris, for call to mind the fate of her sister gods.

"They say to me: 'What strange man are you, to wish us eternal sadness? Would you have us grieve while we starve? Do you not know that work is impossible with a heavy heart and cannot you see that we have lightened our hearts in order to take up the burden our dead broth ers have left to us? What strange man are you?'

"I say to them: 'Europe, it seems to me that you are dancing more than you are working. Too many are living on the blood profits wrung from the slain.'

"They say to me: 'What do you want? We fought well-and we won.'

"I say to them: 'So did Babylon. Yet, though she won, she lost. Guard ye that you do not share her fate.' 11

14

THE GREAT PYRAMID AND THE SPHINX

IT is not an easy matter to get people to understand a subject to which they have given little or no thought whatever; but if one earnestly desires light on a rare and particular subject, as, for instance, the Great Pyramid

and the Sphini, deep concentration is bound to bring results, and the ideas that are the fruit of that "going into the silence;' may be similar to what others have given out and they may be dissimilar. If dissimilar, they may be offered to the earnest, esoteric student, as a working hypo thesis, to be accepted or rejected by him. In case he rejects, reason must be given in order that new light may be shed on the question.

Many scientists have personally studied the Great Pyramid and the Sphinx and made endless measurements. They have arrived, for the most part, at the same conclusion to which that great occultist, Madame Helena P. Blavatsky held, *i. e.,* that "the measuring attainment of the Great Pyramid would indicate all the substance of measure of the heavens and the earth."

So much for that part, but there are other facts to be noted. It will be revealed-and no doubt within a comparatively short time, now-that there are many other secret chambers within this remarkable monument and that its true entrance is from the silent Sphinx. Verily it will not remain silent much longer. That celestial force which conquered the animal nature and resulted in a race of perfected human beings in a far distant Aquarian Age, enabled them to build monuments which would withstand the wear and tear of the ages and be a lode star and a beacon-

light for fellow travelers along the same GREAT PATH-a path that is
narrow and sharp as a razor; a path filled with stones that bruise and cut
the feet. As one persists, the c,tones become fewer; green, velvet grass
and beautiful flowers spring up beside the

W ay, the heart of the aspirant is cheered and strengthened and he
picks himself up again and yet again and goes on with eyes ever
fixed on the flaming star in the distance. And these incomparable monuments show us what was done in past ages, what is being done now,
and what will be accomplished by future generations until all humanity
shall kneel at the feet of *God-ultimate perfection* for all of God's chil-
dren-for we are *all* His.

In the King's chamber, which occupies the highest position therein,
has been found an especially unique object, to which has been given
many names, ranging from sar cophagus to corn-bin.   H. P. Blavatsky
comments caustic ally on the denseness of those who ascribed the latter
name to it, and says it is "a womb within a womb."   It is indeed a sacred chalice, the Holy Grail, and represents the pineal gland within the
head of every human being. This receptacle within the King's chamber
is forever un covered, waiting, patiently, for that precious treasure which
is to rebuild the Sacred Temple.   It is the womb, the
place of conception of the psycho-physical seed.   It is also the tomb of
Joseph, the rock-hewn tomb, in which no man had ever lain, the place to
which the seed returns. Humanity, as a whole, will, from now on, learn
more and more about that wonderful process within the human

body, and more and more will their eyes become opened. Then, indeed, shall we not have definite assurance that the Great Pyramid will
reveal to us the sacred Claustrum and the Door of Brahm?

The sarcophagus, then, was not intended by its per

£ected builders to contain a *dead* body, but a living one, living in the highest sense of the word. It is intended for a lasting memorial, an exemplification ot that birth, life and transmutation of the Savior, the redeemer-the seed, within each human body.

Before entering the King's chamber we find ourselves in an anteroom, wherein "standing aU across the room from the floor to the ceiling" is the strange structure named the "granite leaf." It may well be that these four grooves correspond to the four eminences, the calliculi of the corpora quadrigemina in the mid-brain, the ante chamber of the head.

The King's Chatnber and the Queen's Chamber stand in the same relation *to* each other as do the pineal gland and pituitary body. The King's chamber being placed the highest and likewise the pineal body. No wonder man has considered himself *to* be *above* woman. The Pyramid *well,* which connects the Queen's chamber with the subterranean grotto, corresponds in anatomy *to* the left sympathetic system, and the subterranean grotto is the sacral plexus, where the first crucifixion of the seed (Jesus) takes place. Without a doubt the future will reveal other nd more spacious rooms, corresponding to the organs of the body, and it is remarkable that the chambers which were first revealed to the eyes of hu manity *stand for, and represent those organs within the human body which mankind is destroying in excesses.*

It is no wonder that no trace of any lighting system has been revealed, for no system of lighting was needed. Those perfected builders enjoyed full use of the all-seeing Eye and were a light unto themselves the radiance from that inner eye giving light *to* all that was within the temple.

There was also great wisdom and forethought dis played in closing all the outlets of the Pyramid, all pas sageways-for those Great Ones knew that they were to be submerged, perhaps twice, before the impulse or spirit of the Aquarian Age would impel mankind to obey the inner urge and seek to solve the Pyramid mystery when he himself was beginning to seek and find the solution of the great and wondrous mystery within his own body. Hence passage ways were closed and kept free from the debris of ages.

In this Aquarian Age, this Sun-day of God, when the sign of the Son of man has appeared in the heavens, *all* things will stand revealed. Once again, in the course of the ages will mankind have reached the same goal which the builders of the Great Pyramid reached in that far re mote age of at least *50,000* years. And here and there are found a few whose eyes are beginning to be cleared, whose material vision is being purified, whose brain cells are beginning *to* vibrate *to* that harmony which, to the Ancient Ones, was sweet and thrilling music. And when

this Aquarian Age shall reach its close, we, too, will be able to join in that great anthem of joy and sing the praises of the MOST HIGH-the God within us.

Humanity has been wandering many, many years in the wilderness, but the Promised Land, flowinP. with milk and honey, is very, very near, and soon the 'Stone that the builders rejected will have become the head of the corner."

15

ISAIAH

" **A**nd in that day shall there be an altar to the Lord in the midst of the land of Egypt, and a pillar at the border thereof to the Lord."

-Isaiah 19:19.

. SAIAH in Hebrew means "Salvation of Jehovah" and

I   Jehovah means the whole body of man, but more especially does it mean the second man Adam, a

quickening spirit, the Lord God from heaven, the "I AM THE LORD THY GOD."

The geography of Upper Egypt and Lower Egypt resembles the anatomy of man's body. The solar plexus is the dividing line between the lower, ani-mal (Latin for bad life) or Adam-earthly man and the spiritual Ego residing in the heart-shaped cerebellum (see chart). "As a man thinketh in his heart so is he." The Ego thinks where it resides.

The *salvation* of the Ego is in the "midst of Egypt," etc.

In the archives of ancient Egypt, two crowns have

been found, one white, representing Upper Egypt, and the other red, representing Lower Egypt. Comment is un necessary.

The Great Pyramid is situated exactly on the geo graphical center between Upper and Lower Egypt. Thus it is "In the *midst* of Egypt as a whole and "on the bor ders thereof," of both sections.

The Pyramid of Cheops is an encyclopedia of physical science and astral lore. The science of numbers, weights, measures, astronomy, astrology and the secret mysteries of physiology are symboled in that incomparable monu ment. The history of Freemasonry is recorded there. Note on chart the descen·t of spinal cord, the pneumogas tric nerve, the two wonderful cords of nerves, Adi and Pingala and their relation *to* **NUN,** in Bethlehem, and you will find by the study of books on them that the pas-

sage ways correspond to the inner man and typifies the mysterious Hiram Abiff by whose death the *Word* was lost and finally restored by his resurrection.

The Pyramid, the altar in the midst of Egypt, was reared by people who lived in some former Day of Judg ment, some past Aquarian Age, and who possessed wis dom that enabled them to solve the mystery of Christ hid in God-"The seed is the WORD of God."

$ $ $

FROM "THE GREAT PYRAMID JEEZAH"

By Louis P. McCARTY

"**THE** author believes that no man can study the Bible a great while, carefully and dispassionately noting its place in the world, its surround-ings, its

handings down, its prophetical bearings, not considered in detail, but in their large and comprehensive scope, with out coming to the con-viction that a divine power and providence doth in some way hedge it about, and without coming to the conviction that this divine power is a conscious entity, just as we are; that he is, by his superiority, wisdom and power, continually and everywhere, intelli gently present as the *im-mediate cause* of each sequence in all the universe, however minute."

16

THE OPTIC THALAMUS

THE LAMP OR EYE

"**THE** THALAMUS," within which is the Optic, or eye, "is the great ganglion of the inter-brain. It is called the bed or chamber. It projects back

ward over the mid-brain. Laterally, it rests against the superior lamina of the internal capsule, which separates it from the *lentiform* nucleus. It is shaped like an egg, with the small end directed forward. It measures 4 cm. or about one and a half inches in length, and 2.5 cm. or one inch in width and thickness. It has an anterior and posterior extremity arid four *surfaces."-Santee.*

"The posterior surface (dorsal) of the mid-brain, though free, is entirely concealed by the cerebellar and cerebral hemispheres. It forms part of the floor of the transverse fissure of the cerebrum and is covered by pia mater. The lateral sulcus bounds it on each side. From the sulcus laterals it elevates abruptly toward the median line, where it presents a longitudinal groove. This pro duces two ridges which are subdivided by a transverse groove into *FOUR EMINENCES* (see article on The Great Pyramid and the Sphinx), the colliculi of the cor pora quadrigemina. On either side, anterior and a little lateral to the quadrigeminal bodies, is the medial genicu late joined to the inferior quadrigeminal colliculus by an oblique ridge, called the brachium inferius. The nearly parallel longitudinal ridges below the corpora quadrige mina are formed by the brachia conjunctiva of the cere bellum. The bottom of the groove between them is formed by the superior medullary velum of Vieussens, when the trochlear nerve (fourth), is seen issuing.

Mid-Brain

1. Corpora quadrigernina and brachia.
2. Pedunculi
1. Tegrnenta.
2. Substantia nigra.
3. Bases pedunculi.

" The four colliculi of the corpora quadrigemina and the four brachia connecting them with the geniculate bodies constitute the quadrigeminal lamina, which forms the greater part of the posterior surface of the mid-brain. It is also called the tectum. This lamina rests upon the dorsum of the pedunculi cerebri. The lamina quadrige mina presents a small median triangle between the su perior colliculi and the habenula, called the subpineal triangle, in which the pineal body rests. The lamina is invested with pia mater."

All the above is taken from Santee's "Anatomy of the Brain and Spinal Cord." He is an authority on this subject.

"The ancients, from time immemorial, have considered the pine tree as the most sacred of all trees. The pineal gland or Corpus pineale, is shaped like the pine cone, and the ancient physiologist who gave it its name, must as suredly have understood its great esoteric function. It is 6 mm. (*0.25* inches) high, and 4 mm. (0.17 inches) in diameter, joined to the roof of the third ventricle by a flatteqed stalk, the habenula. It is also called epiphysis and conarium. It is small, reddish and the size of a pea. Its interior is made up of closed follicles surrounded by in-growths of connective tissue. The follicles are filled with epithelial cells mixed with *calcareous* (lime) matter, the *brain-sand* (acervulus cerebri). Calcareous deposits are found also on the pineal stalk and along the choiroid *plexuses.*"-Santee. This organ is Mars-Uranus in as tronomical correspondence.

Let us examine, for a moment.1. the wonderful term "pia mater."

What marvelous light floods the mind of the esoteric student when once the real meaning of this term becomes clear. Pia mater is Latin for *"tender mother."* It is the inner and most vascular (full of vessels) of the three membranes of the brain and spinal cord. The spinal fluid comes from the pia mater of the *cerebrum,* and this fluid, Santee tells us, "is more like *tears and sweat,* than serum." These fluids are both saline and alkaline, there being a large per cent of sodium chloride therein.

The wonderful pia mater, or tender mother, is the mother substance, the pure water, the Virgin Mary, the immaculate mother of all things. Most truly was Mary, the Mother of God, a spiritual as well as a physiological and chemical truth.

The Pituitary Body is given this name because it se cretes a mucus or phlegm. It is a small, reddish, ellipsoid organ in a depression of the sphenoid bone, and attached to the brain by a peduncle. "It contains a viscid, jelly like material (pituita), which suggested the name. It is also called tl{e hypophysis. It consists of two lobes bound together by connective tissue, and in structure resembles the thyroid gland. The anterior lobe is hollowed out on its posterior surface (kidney-shaped) and receives the posterior lobe, the infundibulum, into the cavity. (The infundibulum is a *funnel-shaped passage-a* canal from this body (pituitary) to the third ventricle.) This body secretes a fluid that seems to stimulate the growth of con nective tissues and to be essential to sex development." *Santee.* This organ has a Mars-Neptune correspondence.

The pineal gland is the male spiritual organ-the elec tric body. Otherwise called "Joseph" in Bible terminol ogy. The Father of Jesus-the male element in the seed

-the source of the seed. To it, also, the seed, or Jesus, the Son, returns after his work is done. Joseph of Ari mathaea receives the body of J <;.sus and lays it in *his own* rock hewn tomb "wherein no man was ever laid before." The pineal gland becomes hard like a rock when the "brain-sand," the saved seed, is furnished it. When no material is being returned in tithes to the brain, the pineal body is flabby and pasty.

Let us examine, for a moment, those organs above the optic thalamus. In the article on Santa Claus, the Island of Reil and the claustrum have been described.

It is interesting to note that there are five different bodies lying in a perpendicular line directly beneath the suture, as follows : First, the Island of Reil; the claus trum ; the external capsule; the lentiform nucleus, and the internal capsule. Directly beneath the latter is the thalamus.

The internal capsule is a funnel-like group of nerve fibers which enter the cerebrum and are reinforced by a great number of additional fibers from the thalamus, which converge upward. The bell of this funnel opens upward and contains the *lentiform nucleus.* L

"The lentiform nucleus occupies the cone like cavity of the internal capsule, by whose laminae it is separated from the ventricle.
IT RESEMBLES A BI-CONVEX LENS with a somewhat thickened anterior border, when viewed in horizontal section.   It is triangular in shape. The hypothenuse and base are formed, respectively, by the superior and inferior laminae of the internal capsule. The external capsule forms the perpendicular and sepa rates the lentiform nucleus from the *claustrum.*"-*Santee.* We can easily see, from the above description of the organs, that they are corelated and form the path from the thalamus to the "door of Brahma." It is through this channel that the attenuated, ethereal substance from without is conveyed to the inner eye. The rays, or vibrations, which converged along this pathway are, by means of the lentiform nucleus, the bi-convex lens in the cere

brum, focalized in the "ALL-SEEING EYE."

Wonder of all wonders is the head of man, within which the Adam-man and the God-man dwells-Taurus and Aries, the house and the temple.

"If a man cannot *rule* his own house, how can he *take*
care of the *church* (temple) of *God?*"

17

CENTRAL EYE

"And the lamp thereof is the *lamb.*"-Rev.

HE optic thalamus, the central eye, in the center of the head, is called both "lamp" and "lamb."

The thalamus ("chamber") is a mass of gray matter at the base of the cerebrum, projecting into and bounding the third ventricle.

The Hebrew letters, Lamed, Aleph, Mem and Beth mean, in their order, "overcoming," "father," "mother" and "house," or some material-ized form.

While "p" in "lamp" gives a different meaning. P, from the seven-teenth letter of the Hebrew alphabet, "pe" means "speech," or that which radiates or goes forth. In the Tarot it is referred to as "The force which dis penses the essence of life, which gives it the means of perpet-ually renewing its creations after destruction." One may speak destruc-tively and then, having seen the light, is able to speak constructively.

Thus we see how it also means rays or light, etc., etc., hence LAMP.

The essence of life within us, the *oil,* is what feeds this lamp or causes it to give light-if it is carried up to the place where this lamp or candle, which the Bible refers to, is, which is the optic within the thalamus, re-ferred to above.

"If thine eye be single ('free from defect'-Dictionary)

thy whole body will be full of light."

The outer eyes see only by reflection. The vibrations from the inner eye, optic, is conveyed along the optic nerves and produced, spectacular, on the ether.

Thus we, frequently, when trying to comprehend some thing, put our hand over our eyes for a moment and then exclaim, "Oh, yes, now I see."

"Behold the lamb of God *which* taketh away the sins of the world."

The seed is also referred to as the lamb, as it is neces sary for the seed or Jesus to be carried up into this part of the anatomy, in order that it may cause the optic to vibrate rapidly, and thus produce the illumination. "We shall be changed in the twinkling of an eye."

Exodus 15 :26, "If thou wilt diligently hearken to the voice of the Lord thy God, and wilt do that which is right in his sight, and wilt give ear to his commandments, and keep all his statutes, I will put none of these diseases upon thee, which I have brought upon the Egyptians; for I am the Lord that healeth thee.

Psalms 25 :1, "Unto thee O Lord, do I lift up my soul."

25:13, "His soul shall dwell at ease; and his seed shall inherit the earth." •

Psalms 37 :1-5, "Fret not thyself because of evildoers, neither be thou envious against the workers of iniquity. "For they shall soon be cut down like the grass, and

wither as the green herb.

"Trust in the Lord and do good; so shalt thou dwell in the land, and verily thou shalt be fed.

"Delight thyself also in the Lord, and he shall give thee the desires of thine heart.

"Commit thy way unto the Lord; trust also in Him; and He shall bring it to pass.

"And He shall bring forth thy righteousness as the light, and thy judgment as the noonday.

"The steps of a good man are ordered by the Lord; and He delighteth in his way.

"Though he fall he shall not be utterly cast down, for the Lord upholdeth him with His hand.

"Depart from evil and do good and dwell forever more.

"Mark the *perfect* man and behold the upright; for the end of that man is peace."

Psalms 62: 1-2, "Truly my soul waiteth upon God; from Him cometh my salvation.

"He only is my rock and my salvation; He is my defense; I shall not be greatly moved."

I

Psalms 91, "He that dwelleth in the secret place of the Most High shall abide under the shadow of the Almighty. "He shall cover thee with His feathers and under His wings shalt thou trust; His truth shalt be thy shield and

buckler.

"Thou shalt not be afraid for the terror by night; nor for the arrow that flieth by day.

"Nor for the pestilence that walketh in darkness; nor for the destruction that wasteth by noonday.

"There sh'all no evil befall thee.   Neither shall any plague come nigh thy dwelling.

"For he shall give his angels charge over thee, to keep thee in all thy ways."

Psalms 103 :5, ".Who satisfieth thy mouth with good things; so that thy youth is ren-ewed like the eagles."

Psalms 119 :105 NUN, "Thy word is a lamp unto my feet and a light unto my path."

Psalms 127 :1, "Except the Lord build the house, they labor in vain that build it."

Psalms 132 :11, "Of the fruit of thy body will I set upon thy throne."

St. Luke 12 :31, "But rather seek ye the Kingdom of God; and all these things shall be added to you."

18

THE PHYSIOLOGICAL
STATEMENT

EXTRACTS FROM A PAPER BY PROF. SMILEY
(Lately of Cornell University)

HE sacral region of man's body, near the base of the spinal column, is a gland larger than a hen's egg, of spongy character, and into which is secreted, trom

the blood, a small amount of oil, at the same time that the blood throws out refuse into the bladder.

Exceedingly little has been known to physiologists about this gland, or about the purpose of the secretion, except that in elderly men it often becomes the seat of a disease called prostitis, and that in young men of dissolute habits the secretion becomes filthy.

This gland is known in the East as the Kundalini, and in the New Testament, Greek, as the Kardia.

It will be best to know it here by that name, rather than by the medical term. The oil in it will elsewhere be iden tified with the Greek psyche, and be so referred to herein.

The oil is subject to very varied degrees of consistency; from very thin, volatile oil that promptly evaporates when exposed to the air, to one having a good body, a truly fixed oil, that will form a permanent stain upon a piece of paper. In the most healthy, wise and vigorous men, it is a fixed oil. In the average kind of man to be met on the street, it is more or less volatile. In "rakes" it is very malodorus and may contain pus.

For its highest and purest condition when it is a fixed oil, colorless, odorless and tasteless or sweet, not really acid, nor really alkaline, we shall use the Greek term Chrism, or for short, by the root letters 9f the noun for oil, and of the verb, to oil-Chri-in Greek XPI.

It is necessity of nature that the oil, when purified or secreted in the Kardia shall usually make its way out again through the capillaries into the blood and so pass all over

I the body, wherever the blood goes. It 1s, then, one of the constituents of the blood. "The blood of Christ."

At the present day, boys fifteen years old and older, usually get more or less annoyed by nature's complaints of the congestion. Indeed, it appears in boys seven to four teen years old-a proof that this annoyance does not come from the seminal vesicles. Every cigarette smoker gets a certain relief from smoking, because the poisonous and narcotic effect of the tobacco deadens the voice of nature.

It has been proven that when this gland and its oil act properly, there is not only *no desire for tobacco,* but *tobacco is then too repulsive to be tolerated for a moment.* The BODY IS A LAMP.   THIS OIL IS ITS

ILLUMINATING SUBSTANCE. WITHOUT IT THERE IS NO CONSCIOUSNESS. WHEN IT IS COMPLETELY EXHAUSTED, CONSCIOUS NESS CEASES AND DISINTEGRATION TAKES PLACE.

This oil is not only easily affected, but the effects are carried through the blood into the structure of the tissues of the brain and other parts.

In all ages of the world a small and select few have known how to multiply this life essence.

Of enormous importance is another fact regarding this oil. It is extremely affected by mental states, and by the states of consciousness. The oily milk of a nursing mother may be poisoned by a sudden fit of anger, so as to make her nursing babe sick. This is an effect of mind upon matter. A ferocious appetite can be destroyed in stantly by the reading of a telegram announcing the death of one's mother.

The physiological results of having plenty of good oil thus circulated constantly in the body we have demon strated to be:

First: Destruction o_f all semblance of nervousness, irritability, greed, fear and unrest.

Second: The perfection of digest on and assimilation. Third: Restoration of impaired eyesight and hearing.

Prevention of decay in the teeth.

Fourth: Full amount of the most enjoyable and restful sleep. Freedom from the use of all drugs. Much less food is desired or needed. There is no demand for stimulants.

Fifth: Neutralization of blood poisoning. Probable destruction of cancerous and all other blood diseases.

Sixth: Prompt and complete prevention of all kinds of self-abuse. Restoration from the effects of earlier in discretions.

Seventh: Immunity from colds and probably from all kinds of infectious diseases.

Eighth: Restoration of youthful vigor and prevention of all frailities of old age.

Ninth: In short-accomplishment of everything that unlimited vitality should be expected to produce.

19

THE WIVES AND CHILDREN OF JACOB OR ISRAEL

JACOB means "heel-catcher," hence circle. The name Jacob, or Jacob's ladder, is applied to the twelve signs of the Zodiac, and the sign Aries, the head, and Pisces, the feet, represent the point of contact, the place

where the circle joins.

In his dream Jacob saw the heavens open and God let down a ladder, and the angels (angles) of God descending and ascending upon it. God promised him that his seed should be as the dust of the earth, and in him all families of the earth should be blessed. God promised to be with him and to bring him *again* to the land whereon the promise was made.

On awakening from his sleep Jacob said, "This is none other but the house of God and this is the gate of heaven." The name of the place was called Bethel (House of the Sun). And Jacob promised to give *one tenth* of all that he should receive, unto the Lord. (See Tithes).

This story is one of the most remarkable and significant of all of the Biblical allegories, since it must be applied cosmically as well as microcosmically.   It represents the solar plexus in man-and the zodiac in the solar system. We can easily understand the meaning of Jacob's journey, and how, in process of time he came to l\1ount Peniel (pineal gland) where he wrestled with the angel of God, who blessed him and changed his name to Israel. He had then *come again* to the place from which he had started for he had again seen God face to face.   It means that the circle was complete-Jacob had caught hold *of* his

own heel.

The bread that he was to eat was the seed born or formed in the center of the circle-the solar plexus, and,

of course, stands for the cosmic sun also, the savior of the world. This bread or seed was to become the savior of the Adam-man.

It is very evident that the "Old" Testament referred more especially to the cosmic processes; the "New" Testament to those same processes *within* man, since "as above, so below." There is nothing in the universe that is not within man.

Jacob was commanded to go and seek out Laban (white) and to marry one of his daughters. Therefore, the circle of the Zodiac proceeded to that part of the heavens called the "milky way," and Jacob came upon the daughters of Laban, tending the "flocks." He loved Rachel, for she was beautiful, and he agreed to serve seven years in order to possess her. When the time was up the "marriage" took place, but Jacob found that he had been given Leah, instead of the bride he so desired. The excuse that was given was that Leah was the eldest and hence must be married off first.

Rachel refers to the planet Venus and Leah to the planet Mars. We are told that Leah had "weak eyes," we know that Mars is called the "fiery-eyed." Venus represents love and beauty. Mars also stands for activity, and nothing could be accomplished on this earth by human beings, if there was no active force in mani festation.

Mars has been referred to principally as the planet of war, but we feel that it will not be long before the real nature of Mars will become known. Then will humanity realize that the *same force* that is manifested in war and brutality may be transmuted and used in numberless ways for the benefit of humanity. If mankind would use the same amount of force and energy in doing constructive, instead of destructive work, we would soon see Mars through rose-colored glasses, instead of those colored blood-red. Mars means activity, forcefulness, not *necessarily* war or bloodshed. Another great war has been prophtsied because very great activity of Mars is shown, astrologically; but the world is weary, sick unto death of war.

20

THE SOLAR PLEXUS

H OUSES of the Zodiac represented by the twelve children of Jacob (same as Israel).

Benjamin, the thirteen, the Son of the Sun, is Jesus, the fish or seed.

Hebrew, Persian and Syrian names of each house, month or sign.

HEBREW, PERSIAN OR SYRIAN DERIVATIONS QF THE MONJ'HS

	MONTH	SIGN
1st Month:	April, Aries	NISAN: March-April (New day, Passover, Exodus)
2nd Month:	May, Taurus	ZIF: April-May (Flower month, beauty)
3rd Month:	June, Gemini	SIVAN: May-June (Moon)
4th Month:	July, Cancer	TAMMUZ: June-July
5th Month:	August, Leo	AB: July-August

6th Month:	September, Virgo	ELUL: August-September (To glean the vine)

7th Month: October, Libra   ETHANIM: September-Octa-her (Perennial)

8th Month: November, Scorpio   BuL: October-November (Rain)

9th Month: December, SagittariusCHISLEU: November-Decem ber (From Aram, Mars, Orion)

10th Month: January, Capricorn TEBETH: December - Janu ary (Winter)

11th Month: February, Aquarius SEBAT: January-February 12th Month: March, Pisces   ADAR: February-March (Fire-God)

13th or Intercalary Month: VEADAR. (See article on Leap Year.)

As Leah and Rachel, or Mars and Venus, represent activity and love, they also stand for the median line of the Zodiac, for Libra and Aries are ruled by these two planets. Also, these two planets are represented in the head of man, Mars ruling Aries, the upper brain, the Almighty, the *creator* of all, and Venus ruling Taurus, as represented by the cerebellum. The head and the neck rule the body of man. The Adam-man, Taurus or Venus, rules it *if* he has become awakened, when he then becomes the Lord God from heaven, for God is Love. Activity works along wisdom's ways.

Aries and Taurus, represented by Gad and Asher, are the two "lost" tribes ref erred to by so-called Bible stu dents. Lost tribes are not mentioned in the Bible text. They were never lost, but because they are not mentioned many times in connection with the other tribes, or children of Israel, they were *supposed* to have been lost. As they are located in the cerebrum and cerebellum, that part of the anatomy which is *separated* from the torso, we can easily understand the supposition that they were *lost*. Aries and Taurus are the two tribes that lay down the law to the other ten. If the individual lives in excess, saves no seed or oil, these two most important parts of the body *do* become "dead" in trespass and sin, and we say he died of "softening of the brain."

Leah and Rachel, then represent the divisions of the zodiac. From these two wives (and hand-maids) the children, or signs of the zodiac, were produced. These twelve are again divided into the seven and the five. "The seven representing the lunar forces, or seven pneu mata, being differentiations of the 'Great Breath' or 'World Mother,' and symbolized by the Moon. The signs are Cancer, Leo, Scorpio, Virgo, Libra, Sagittarius and *Capricorn.*"-Pryse.

"The five solar forces which pertain to the cerebro spinal system, called the five pranas, or vital airs, or life winds," are represented by Aries, Taurus, Gemini, Pisi:es and *Aquarius.*"-Pryse.

"The four divinities of the zodiac are represented by the Lion, the Bull, the Man and the *Eagle.*-Pryse.

The names of the children of Jacob, or Israel, are given on chart herewith. Benjamin, the only one born in the *promised land.* In Arabia, the blest, was Benjamin, the last and *thirteenth.*

The trials and tribulations of the children of Israel typify the struggle for self-mastery-the harmonizing of all the forces of the body.

The twelve dorsal vertebrae are also esoterically connected with each one of the nerves, ramifying to the solar plexus.

The Hebrew and Syrian names for the different months are also given on the chart.

The youngest child, Benjamin, at whose birth Rachel died, was the Beloved, the tender one, the little one, the ark which the Israelites carried with them on their great Journey.

Rachel died and her "grave is there to this day." Yea, verily in every human being-the seed-pod, the solar plexus center. (See article on Leap Year).

21

PROPHECIES FULFILLED

THE 18th CHAPTER OF REVELATION-MATTHEW, 24th CHAPTER-LUKE, 21st CHAPTER

WE strongly urge our readers to very carefully read all contained in the above chapters, from the view point of astrology, physiology and chemistry.

The zodiacal sign, Aquarius, the man with the pitcher of water is the "sign of the Son of Man in the heavens." The monthly seed is the *Son of Man in* earth, the body.

The fifth son of Jacob (Genesis 29), named Dan, a judge, represents in astrology January 20th to February 22nd, which is the sign Aquarius, and through which the sun passes once yearly.

But the solar system entered that sign on its 2200 year cosmic circle in the year 1900.

As Dan is Hebrew for Judge, and Daniel for wisdom, or *God's* judgment, therefore, earth is *now* in the day or time of judgment.

The great revolutionary planet, Uranus (Ouranous in Greek), the son or sun of heaven, is the ruler of Aquarius and will be regnant for over 2000 years.

For a fulfilled prophecy of the destruction of the com petitive system' of commercialism and the destruction of gold and silver as mediums of exchange, see the 18th Chapter of Revelation. Also, see Russia.

Peter the Great was an Aquarian native, hence Russia will be (is) the first to establish a free Aquarian (wis dom) government.

All who oppose cosmic law are crushed.

"The stars in their course fought for" Russia.

And thus the prophecy, "A nation shall be born in a day" has been fulfilled.

A

KILLING THE FATTED CALF, OR KAPH

IT has been written, the origin of words and the application of the characters differ so widely that "confusion worse confounded" is the result in numberless cases.

The eleverith letter of the Hebrew alphabet is Kaph, a hollow and represents the human hand, a hollow or hal lowed place.

The cerebrum, upper brain, is hollowed and covers the cerebellum like a w_ing. The cerebellum is therefore a secret place where tlie Ego, or spiritual man; the "Second man Adam a quickening spirit," or "The Lord God·from heaven" dwells. (See 91st Psalm).

The upper brain, in the parable of the prodigal son, is represented as the Father, being the cause of and furnish ing the "Substance" to build and replenish the body.

The Ego is represented as saying to the Father, "Give me the portion of goods that falleth to me." Now this portion was the oil that flows do n the Ida and Pingala to form a seed, but the Ego, thinking on the carnal plane "wasted this substance in riotous living." The evil result that fol-lowed is likened to swine, husks, etc., etc.

As in the story of Hiram Abiff in Masonry, after the WORD was lost for a season ("The seed is the WORD"

-Luke) it was resurrected so in the prodigal son parable,

29 . ¾ days passed, the material for another seed de scended and said, "I will *arise* and go to my Father."

When the seed comes forth out of the manger in Beth lehem (house of bread), "*I am* the *bread* of life," a vibra tion of greater life is set up ("Life more abundant"), and it thrills the entire temple of God.

Now comes the astounding revelation:

The original meaning of "kill" is not to take life, neces sarily; it rather means to choke or squeeze. To choke a sponge, or squeeze water from it does not mean to take life, but if one's throat is squeezed or choked for a time and the breath ceases to enter the body, we say the person has been killed.

The gray matter of the upper brain vibrates high-is quickened when "one-tenth is returned to the Lord" and thus secretes more abundantly down to the magnetic, chemical center, the cerebellum called heart in Greek "As a man thinketh in his heart so is he."

So, then, the "Father killed the fatted kaph" for the Son, *i. e.,* gave up life for the Ego. "Hallowed be thy name." The name *is* hollowed, viz., Kaph, a hollow.

The hollow of the knee is named Kaph and spelled calf. Probably it was applied to a young bovine, because of the peculiar hollow of the belly when the animal is very young. Here the reader is_referred to the 91st Psalm. In that marvelous allegory, or epic, the hollow of the

"Most High" is represented as casting a shadow for the Ego in the "Secret place." (See cerebellum in chart).

"His feathers shall cover thee." Note the resemblance of the brain convolutions to feathers.

22

THE ANTI-CHRIST

PRIMITIVE Christians, the Essenes, fully realized and taught the great truth t at Christ was a sub stance, an oil or ointment contained especially in the Spinal Cord, consequently in all parts of the body, as every nerve in the body is directly or indirectly connected with the wonderful "River that flows out of Eden (the

upper brain) to water the garden."

The early Christians knew that the Scriptures, whether written in ancient Hebrew or the Greek, were allegories, parables or fables·based on the human body, "fearfully and wonderfully made."

These adepts knew that the secretion (gray matter creative) which issues (secretes), from the cerebrum, was the source and *cause* of the physical expression called *man;* and they knew that the "River of Jordan" was symbolized in the spinal cord and that the "Dead Sea" was used to symbolize the Sacred Plexus at the base of the spinal column where the Jordan (spinal cord) ends, typifying the entrance of Jordan into the Dead Sea.

The thick, oily and salty substance composing the Sacral Plexus, "Cauda Equina" (tail of the horse), may be likened unto crude Petroleum (Petra, mineral, or salt, and oleum-Latin for oil) and the thinner substance, oil or ointment in the spinal cord, may be compared with coal oil; and when this oil is carried·up and *crosses* the Ida and Pingala (two *fluid nerves* that end in a *cross* in medulla oblongata where it contacts the cerebellum (Gol gotha-the *place of the skull)-this* fluid is *refined,* as coal oil is *refined,* to produce gasoline-a higher rate of motion that causes the ascension of the airship.

| 97 |

When the oil (ointment) is *crucified-(* to crucify means to *increase* in power a thousand *fold-not to kill)* it remains two days and a half, (the moon's period in a sign) in the tomb (cerebellum) and on the third day ascends to the Pineal Gland that connects the cerebellum

W ith the Optic Thalmus, the Central Eye in the Throne of God that is the chamber overtopped by the hollow (hallowed) ca used by the curve of the cerebrum (the "Most High" of the body) which is the "Temple of the Living God," the living, vital substance which is a precipi tation of the "Breath of Life" breathed into man therefore, the "Holy (whole) Ghost" or breath.

The Pineal Gland is the "Pinnacle of the Temple." The modus operandi by which the oil of the spinal cord reaches the Pineal Gland is described in what follows. "There is no name under Heaven whereby ye may be saved except Jesus Christed and then crucified" (correct rendering of the Greek text).

Every twenty-nine and one-half days, when the moon is in the sign of the zodiac that the sun was in at the birth of the native, there is a seed, or Psycho-Physical germ born *in* the, or *out of,* the Solar Plexus (the Manger) and this seed is taken up by the nerves or branches of the Pneumo gastric nerve, and becom s the "Fruit of the Tree of Life," or the "Tree of good and evil"-viz.: *good,* if *saved* and "cast upon the waters" (circulation) to reach the Pineal Gland; and *evil,* if *eaten* or consumed in sexual expression on the physical plane, or by alcoholic drinks, or glut-tony that causes ferment-acid and even alcohol in intestinal tract-thus-"No drunkard can inherit the Kingdom of Heaven" *for acids and alcohol cut, or chem ically split, the oil that unite! with the mineral salts in the body and thus produces the monthly seed.*

This seed, having the odor of fish, was called Jesus, from Ichtos (Greek for fish) and Nun (Hebrew for fish)-thus "Joshua the son of

Nun,"-"I am the bread of life;" "I am the bread that came down from heaven;" "Give us this day our daily bread."

The fruit of the Tree of Life, therefore, is the "Fish bread" of which thou shalt not eat on the plane or animal or Adam (earth-dust of the earth plane) : but to "Him that overcometh will I give to eat of the fruit of the Tree of Life," because he saved it and it returned to him in the cerebellum, the home of the Spiritual mia,n, the Ego.

The cerebellum is heart-shaped and called the heart in Greek-thus "As a man thinketh in his heart so is he."

The bodily organ that men in their ignorance call heart is termed divider or pump in Greek and Hebrew. Our blood divider is not the button that we touch when we think, but it is the upper lobe of cerebellum that vibrates thought. The lower lobe is the animal (mortal) lobe that governs the animal world-that section of the body *below the* Solar Plexus, called lower Egypt-natural body kingdom of earth-Appollyon-the Devil (lived, spelled backward) Satan (Saturn governs the bowels), etc.

Fire and Brimstone (the lake of fire) comes from the fact that sulpliur (brimstone) is the prime factor in generating the rate of motion called heat, and *overeating* develops a surplus of sulphur.

During the first 300 years of the Christian era all that has been above written was understood by the real Christians, and about the end of that time the persecution of these Essenes by the priesthood became so marked that they met in secret and always made the sign of the fish.

About the year *325,* Constantine, the pagan Roman Emperor, called the teachers of Christianity together at Nicea.

Constantine murdered his mother and boiled his wife in oil because they still held to the original doctrines of the Essenes. Constantine was told by the Priests of his time that there was no forgiveness for crimes such as his, except through a long series of incarnations; but the anti Christ sought to concoct a plan by which he hoped to cheat the Cosmic law.

And so it came to pass, after months of wrangling and fighting over the writings of the primitive Christians who clothed the wonders of the human body in oriental imagery, that the council, sometimes by a bare majority vote, decided which of the manuscripts were the "Word of God" and which were not.

The very important point in the minds of those ignor ant priests-whether or no an angel had wings-was decided in favor of wings by three majority. The minority contended that, as Jacob let down a ladder for angels to descend and ascend upon it was prima facie evidence that angels do not have wings.

Just think, for a moment, upon the colossal ignorance of these priests who did not know that Jacob in Hebrew means "heel catcher" or circle, and that ladder referred to the influence of the signs of the zodiac upon the earth; and as one sign rising every two hours forms a circle every twenty-four hours (the four and twenty Elders of Revelation) the outer stars of the rising suns (sons) ∴ "catching on" to the last sons (suns) of the sign ascend ing.

But now we come to the anti-Christ:

The council of Nicea, dominated by Constantine, *voted* that the symbols of the human body were persons; that Jesus was a certain historical man, a contention utterly and indubitably without foundation, in fact, and that all who *believed* (?) the story would be *saved* and *forgiven here* and *now*. The idea appealed to Constan tine as an easy way out of his troubled mind and so the scheme of salvation by the actual blood of a real man or god was engrafted in the world.

Constantine and his dupes saw that the only way to perpetuate the infamy was to keep the world in ignorance of the operation of the Cosmic Law, so they *changed* "Times and seasons."

The date that they made the sun enter Aries was March 21st. Why? March 21st *should* be the *first* day of Aries, the head; April 19th should be the first day of Taurus, the neck, and so on through the twelve signs; but these designing schemers knew that by thus suppressing the truth the people might come to realize what was meant by "The heavens declare the glory of God."

Again: the moon, in its *monthly* round of 29¼ days

enters the outer stars (or suns) of a constellation two and one-half days before it enters the central suns of the constellations that are known as the Signs of the Zodiac or the "Circle of Beasts." But even unto this day the whole anti-Christ world (so-called "Christian") except the astrologers, go by almanacs that make the moon enter a sign of the zodiac two and one-half days before it does enter it and thus perpetuate the lie of the pagan Constantine, the anti-Christ.

23

WHAT SO-CALLED CHRISTIANS SAY, AND THE ANSWER

"Christ was a man, born of a woman." "We believe in Jesus, we expect to die and then•be saved." "Jesus is greater than man." "Only Jesus was conceived of the Holy Ghost."

"We will go to heaven when we die." •,

"The earth will be destroyed." "I believe in Jesus."

"I am born of God."

"Jesus Christ is a man, a Savior that died and went away and will come again."

Jesus was born, conceived of the Holy Ghost (Ghost is "breath" in Greek-the *whole* breath, or air breathed in.

"He that believeth in me shall never die." Death is an enemy to be overcome."

"All that I do ye can do." "Know ye not that the Holy Ghost dwelleth in you?"

"The Kingdom of Heaven is within you."   "Thy will be done in earth as it is in Heaven." "The earth endureth forever." "These *signs shall follow those* who believe in me," etc., etc. "He that is born of God will not sin, for his seed remaineth in him."

"He that confesseth not that Jesus Christ *is come in the ftesh (your* flesh), the same is an Anti-Christ. That means, one opposed to the truth that there is a seed born in you from the Christ (oil) in you. "And unto thee and *thy seed,* which is Christ."-Pau/.

For more evidence that Jesus and Christ are in *your flesh* see 1st Epistle of John-4th Chapter, 2nd and 3rd verses.

The Greek and Hebrew texts of our Scriptures plainly teach that Jesus and Christ, John and baptism, cruci fixion and ascension, the triumph of the Ego over the "Enemy death" are in the substance and potentialities of the body; and that these fluids can and will save the physical body, if conserved and not consumed (or wasted) in sexual or animal desire.

All of whatever name or religious denomination who teach a contrary doctrine agree with Constantine who

appeared in the "Latter days" of the Pure Christian Practice.

Who is the anti-Christ? Look at a world of ruins.

Does a good tree bring forth evil fruit?

The so-called teachers of, and believers in Christian ity believe as Constantine and his priests, that Christ is "out in the desert" of the Judean hills-out on Calvary. Do they ever look for the meaning of Calvary in Greek? Calvary means a *skull,* and Golgotha-the *place* of the skull, exactly where the seed is crucified.

One-half of the combatants in the world's Armaged don have been praying, as Constantine prayed, "for God's help for Christ's sake." The other half pray *to* the same imaginary God and Christ out in "The desert" of *their own ignorance* for "peace and victory."

Return and come unto the God and Christ *within you,*

oh I ye deluded ones, and the bugles will all sing truce along the iron front of war and the "Ransomed of the Lord will return *to* Zion with songs and everlasting joy upon their faces."

24

THE RIB-LAH THAT MADE THE
WOM(B)MAN

FOR the Lord hath created a *new* thing *in* the earth. A woman shall compass a *man."-Jere miah 31;22.*

"And she brought forth a *man* child." *See Revelation 12th, Chapters 1 to 6.*

"Rib-lah, the eastern boundary of Israel." It was between Shepham and the Sea of Chinnereth (Gennes aret)".-*Smith's Bible Dictionary.* This was the place of the "Holy Fountain."

"But when the fullness of time was come, God sent forth his Son, made of a woman, made under the law."

-Galatians 4;4.

The children of Israel (warriors of God-see Smith's Bible Dictionary), are the thirteen seeds. (See Jacob's Children-name changed to Israel) .

There is no historical Land of Israel. The name is found first in the Secret or Sacred writings which pertain to the *inner* functions of the human body-purely chem ical and physiological.

Sacred-from "sacral," refers to the lower part of the spinal column.

Secret, from secretion, gray matter or oil from the upper brain, the fountain of life, the "Secret place of the Most High"-the *heaved* up place, the heaven within us.

N, the fourteenth letter of the Hebrew alphabet, added to *heave*, makes it heaven, because the seed, the fish which N, Nun, the fourteenth letter represents, on being carried to the pineal gland regenerates the in dividual, and the upper brain becomes a manifested heaven. This seed "Seeks the kingdom of heaven."

There is probably no definite trace of the semi-lunar ganglion, two half moon-shaped ganglion near the sup

r arenal glands, situated near the kidneys, that connect the spinal cord at the twelfth dorsal vertebra with the solar plexus, in the body of an infant, yet it is quite probable, if not certain, that the vestigal form, power and potency is implanted there at birth.

When the boy or girl reaches "about twelve," the semilunar and the manger (or nun) in Bethlehem is in full function, and hence Jeremiah's declaration.

It is evident that the fluids, creative, omnipotent, *flow* ing "Out of Eden to water the garden" *(Gen. 2:10), creates a new thing in the earth- the* body, about that age, using the *rib-lah* to make the woman or worn (b) an, or womb *in mankind-male* or female.

This womb *does* compass circle a man (child-seed), "The seed is the Son of man." Again, "Know ye not that the Son of man hath power *in earth* to forgive sin?" Analysis of "man," according to the Jewish Kaballah, reveals the fact that M, the thirteenth letter of the alpha bet, means woman, mother, and is written thus, "mem."

A, the first letter-Aleph, means father or male strength or forces.

Nun, the fourteenth letter of the alphabet, means fruit, son, child, savior that redeems, therefore, man is mother, first (or Mary), then father, then son-redeemer, hence destined to be ultimately *saved.*

The sun and moon (see Joshua commanding the sun to stand still) and the pneumogastric or vagus nerve, the spinal cord and all that portion of the body *above* the median line, the "Middle wall of partition," is exactly the *same* in man and woman, and the functions in the "king dom," in *each* body, enables them, separately and *alone*, to "work out their own salvation, or secretions. (See Joseph and Mary), the pineal gland and pituitary body, *both* in *one* human organism, thus; "In my kingdom (saith the seed), there is no marrying nor giving in marriage."

Note: Rib-lah, the *eastern* boundary of Israel: The

back is called the East, front, West; feet, South (down South), head, North (up north) , hence the semilunar g-an,zlion is *East* of Israel, the *regenerative womb in man. See chart.*

According to Hindu secret writings, God took a rib out of the female to make the male. Literally speaking, this idea would be much more reasonable than a literal rendering of the passage in Genesis.

"A woman hid a little leaven in a bag of meal and it leavened the whole lump."

Woman, or the *womb in man,* the upper or regenerative womb. Leaven, or yeast, the seed that comes forth from the womb in man, expands or causes the oil in the spinal cord (the "bag of meal"), to multiply. See loaves and fishes in the gospel. Also "Give one-tenth (tithes) to the Lord."

No wonder David-the Seed-is made to say of the man whose delight is in God: "And in thy law will I meditate day and night.

25

THE BRIDGE OF LIFE

A "C onceived in sin and brought forth in iniquity."
NOISELESS, patient spider,
I mark'd, where, on a little promontory, it stood, isolated;

M ark'd how, to explore the vacant, vast surrounding,
It launch'd forth filament, filament, filament, out of itself;
Ever unreeling them-ever tirelessly speeding them.
"And you, 0 my soul, where you stand,
Surrounded, surrounded, in measureless oceans of space,
Ceaselessly musing, venturing, throwing-seeking the spheres, to connect them ;
Till the bridge you will need, be form'd-till the ductile anchor hold;
Till thegossamer thread you fling, catch somewhere, **0** my soul."
-*Walt Whitman.*
"**O** Man of Earth, watch well the steps thou findest, Spread out before thy feet by cosmic plan;
Do thy soul's best, with body and with mind,
To pay thy debt, and bridge this Karmic Span."
-*Edith F. A. U. Painton.*

The statement of Holy Writ, that "man is conceived in sin and brought forth in iniquity" has a three-fold mean ing, viz., chemical, physiological and astrological. The real meaning in the original is, that the hum n embryo remains nine months in the female laboratory, thus fall ing short three months of completing a solar or soul year. It also represents the journey of the ego from the moon to earth, or conception. Twelve, which represents the circle and stands for completion.

The word sin comes from Schin, the twenty-first letter of the Hebrew alphabet, and means to fall short of com pleteness, or understanding, wisdom. In the Tarot sym bol, S, or Sin, is represented by the "Blind Fool," one lacking in wisdom, "Brought forth in iniquity" is merely a repetition of the words "born in sin." Iniquity and

i nequity or unequal, ean the same. The ancient He brews called Moon, Sin, because it gave light only part of the time.

To acquire wisdom that will enable the Ego in flesh to build a bridge across the three-month gap, or space between the point of conception and birth, is the one real problem that confronts the ego on the material plane of expression. The alchemists, seers and astrolo ians of all ages have wrestled with this problem in their ceaseless endeavors to unravel the great mystery of man's dominion over flesh. Whether it be the chemist seeking new com pounds, the physiologist searching and testing the fluids of the fearfully and wonderfully made body of man, the alchemist probing for the Elixir of Life-the Ichor of the Gods or the astrologian pulling and adjusting the etheric wires that criss-cross the spaces in an earnest desire to make good and sane the statement "The wise man rules his stars,"-all, all are seeking to span the awful space that yawns between the neophyte and the Promised Land of imlmortality in the body, where "in my flesh I shall see God," and when and where he can truly say with the regenerated Job, "I have heard of thee by the hearing of the ear, but now mine eye seeth thee." Man must work out his own salvation.

The bridge to be built across the three-months space must have a mineral base or rock foundation. "Thou art Peter (petra, stone, or mineral) , on thee will I build my church," etc. Church is from the second Hebrew letter, Beth, a house temple, or church. The human body is a house, temple, or church for the Soul which may be lost or saved by the higher self or spiritual ego residing in the cerebellum the "Secret Place of the Most High." "Know ye not that your bodies are the temple (church) of God?"

There are twelve inorganic mineral cell-salts in the human body, and these minerals (stones in the temple) correspond in vibration to the twelve signs of the Zodiac. During the nine m;onths of gestation the embryo receives and appropriates the creative energies of nine of these salts, leaving three to be supplied after the parting of the umbilical cord. Take for example a native born Febru-

a ry 22nd, with the Sun's entry into Pisces: The embryo, having begun its journey at the gate of Gemini and nego tiated the nine gestatory signs, his blood vibration at birth is thus deficient in the qualities of Pisces, Aries and Taurus, as also in the chemical dynamics of phosphate of iron, phosphate of potassium and sulphate of sodium- the mineral bases respectively of the signs of this uncom pleted quadrant. In so far as his circulatory system may receive these needed builders, the health will be balanced and life prolonged.

The chemical union of these cell-salts with organic matter, such as oil, fibrin, albumen, etc., forms the various tissues of the body and administers to the physiological needs as represented by the Bridge, that the multiple cells may respond more harmoniously and completely *to* the magic touch of the Divine energy, just as the tones of a musical instrument are made the more melodious through a properly skilled manipulation. And as bridge building in a mechanical sense depends upon the plans and specifications of a competent civil engineer, so does the Bridge of Life depend upon the astrologian to chart and compass the way.

Our diagram indicates at a glance the chemical for mula that appertain respectively to the zodiacal divisions, but to give a clearer conception as regards their specific qualities and physiological action in relation to the various signs, reference may be had *to* the following compend: The coming of Christ and the end of the world has been preached from

every street corner for several years, and thousands are pledging themselves *to* try *to* live as

Christ lived or according *to* their concept of His life.

No great movement of the people ever occurs without a scientific
cause.

The Optic Thalamus, meaning "light of the chamber,"

is the inner or third eye, situated in the center of the head: It connects the pineal gland and the pituitary body. The optic nerve starts
from this "eye single."   "If thine eye be single, thy whole
body will be full of light." The *optic thalamus is the Aries planet* and
when fully developed through physical regeneration it lifts the initi ate
up from the Kingdom of Earth, animal desire below

the solar plexus, to the pineal gland that connects the cerebellum, the
temple of the Spiritual Ego, with the optic thalamus, the third eye.

By this regenerative process millions of dormant cells of the brain are
resurrected and set in operation, and then man no longer "sees through
a glass darkly," but with the Eye of spiritual understanding.

We venture to predict that the planet corresponding to the optic
thalamus will soon be located in the heavens. "The new; order
cometh."   Mars must be dethroned

as ruler of the brain of man.

To those who object to linking chemistry with astrol ogy, the' writer
has this to say:

The Cosmic Law is not in the least disturbed by nega tive statements
of the ignorant individual. Those inves tigators of natural phenomena,
who delve deeply to find Truth, pay little heed to the babbler who says,
"I can't understand how the zodiacal signs can have any relation to the
cell-salts of the human body." The sole reason that he "cannot understand" is because he never tried to understand.

A little earnest, patient study will open the understand ing of any one possessed of ordinary intelligence and make plain the great truth that the UN/verse is what the word implies, i.e., *one verse.*

It logically follows that all parts of one thing are sus ceptible to the operation of any part.

The human body is an epitome of the cosmos.

Each sign of the Zodiac is represented by the twelve functions of the body and the position of the Sun at birth.

Therefore, the cell-salt corresponding with the Sign of the Zodiac and function of the body is consumed more rapidly than other salts and needs an extra amount to supply the deficiency caused by the Sun's influence at that particular time.

In ancient lore Aries was known as the "Lamb of Gad," or God, which represents the head or brain. The brain controls and directs the body and mind of man. The brain itself, however, is a receiver operated upon by celestial influences or angles (angels) and must operate

according to the directing force or intelligence of its source of power.

Man has been deficient in understanding because his brain receiver did not vibrate to certain subtle influences. The dynamic cells in the gray matter of the nerves were not finely attuned and did not respond- hence sin, or falling short of understanding.

From the teachings of the Chemistry of Life we find that the basis of the brain or neyve fluid is a certain mineral salt known as potassium phosphate, or Kali Phos.

.A deficiency in this brain constituent means "sin," or a falling short of judgment or proper comprehension. With the advent of the Aries Lord, God, or planet, cell salts are rapidly coming to the fore as the basis of all healing. Kali phosphate is the greatest healing agent known

to man, because it is the chemical base of material expression and understanding.

The cell-salts of the human organism are now being prepared for use,
while poisonous drugs are being dis carded everywhere. Kali phosphate
is the especial birth salt for those born between March 21 and April 19.

These people are brain workers, earnest, executive and
?etermined-thus do they rapidly use up the brain vital- 1zers.

The Aries gems are amethyst and diamond.

In Bible alchemy Aries represents Gad, the seventh son of Jacob, and
means "armed and prepared"-thus it is said when in trouble or danger,
"keep your head."

In the symbolism of the New Testam nt, Aries corres ponds with the
disciple Thomas. Aries people are natural doubters until they figure a
thing out for them selves.

The astronomer, by the unerring law of mathematics applied to
space, proportion, and the so far discovered wheels and cogs of the uni-
machine, can tell where a cer tain planet must be located before the tele-
scope has veri fied the prediction. So the astro-biochemist knows there
must of necessity be a blood mineral and tissue builder to correspond
with each of the duodenary segments that con stitutes the circle of the
Zodiac.

Not through quarantine, nor disinfectants, nor boards of health,
will man·reach the long-sought plane of physical well-being; nor by de-
nials of disease will bodily regenera tion be wrought; nor by dieting or
fasting or "Fletcher izing" or suggesting, will the Elixir of Life and the
Philosopher's Stone be found. The Mercury of the Sages and the "hidden manna" are not constituents of health foods. Victims of salt baths
and massage are bald before their time, and the alcohol, steam and Turk-
ish bath fiends die young. Only when m;an's body is made chemically
perfect will the mind be able perfectly to ex press itself.

And_,.the secret of this chemical perfectionment is the sum total of the requirements involved in this zodiacal Bridge. The rock-Peter, or Petra-must be completed before the etheric wires that span the gulf between birth forward to the sidereal point of conception can vibrate in such harmony as to sustain the traveller on this "magical bridge of three piers," or the three zodiacal signs through which the material body must successfully function before it may hope to lift the veil of Isis.

The Bridge of Life, a symbol of physical re-genesis, has been exploited in song, drama, and story. Paracel sus, Pythagoras, Lycurgus, Valentin, Wagner, and a long and unbroken line of the Illuminati, from time immem orial have chanted their epics in unison with this "riddle of the Sphinx," across the scroll of which is written, "Solve me, or die."

Of all the multiple adepts or masters that have kept the lights burning above the Three Piers of the magical Bridge, none has more clearly and beautifully written thereof than did the great astrologian poet, Isaiah:

"Then the eyes of the blind shall be opened, and the ears of the deaf shall be unstopped. Then shall the lame man leap as a hart, and the tongue of the dumb shall sing; for in the wilderness shall waters break out, and streams in the desert. And the glowing sand shall become a pool, and the thirsty ground springs of water; in the habitation of jackals, where they lay, shall be grass with reeds and rushes. And a *highway shall be there, and a way and it shall be called, The way of holiness;* the un-

clean shall not *pass over it,* but it shall be for the re deemed; the wayfaring men, yet fools, shall not err therein."

Here we have the last step on the physical plane that breaks down the "middle wall of partition."-Pau/. Then the Ego is enabled to regenerate by saving the Word of God-the Seed-and thus render further m carnations unnecessary.

26

VOL. IV, SACRED BOOKS OF THE EAST

EXTRACTS FROM SEPHER DTZENIOUTHA, OR THE BOOK OF CONCEALED MYSTERY-MEDIEVAL HEBREW

, , **THE** Book of Concealed Mystery" is the book of the ‚equilibrium of balance.

In His form (in the form,' of the Ancient One) existeth the equilibrium.

It is incomprehensible, it is unseen.

The head, which is incomprehensible, is secret in secret.

But it has been formed and prepared in the likeness of a cranium and is filled with crystalline dew.

His skin is of ether, clear and congealed.

His hair is as most fine wool, floating though the balanced equilibrium.

His *eye* is ever open and sleepeth not, for it continually keepeth watch. And the appearance of the lower is according to the aspect of the higher light.

Therein are His two nostrils like mighty galleries, whence His spirit rusheth forth over all. The creative spirit-the "breath of life."

The crystalline dew is the creative lux, or Aur, AVR proceeding from the Limitless One."

Now the author of the "Sepher Dtzenioutha" descend eth to the inferior paths, leaving out Macroprosopus, and examineth the name IHV, YDO HE VAU. In this are represented father and mother and Microprosopus. And first occurreth the supernal I, YOD (the symbol of the father), which is crowned with crown of the *more* Ancient One (that is, whose highest apex denoteth the highest crown, or Macroprosopus; or, according to another read ing of the passage, "which is surrounded by the secret things"-that is, by the influence or beard of Macropo sopus, which covereth both the father and the mother). It is that *membrane of the supernal brain* which, on account of its excellency, both shineth and is concealed."

"In the cranium:" (or skull), Begolgoltha, or in Gol gotha. In the New Testament it is worthy of note that Jesus Christ (the Son) is said to be crucified at Golgotha (the skull) ; while here, in the Kabbalah, Mircoproso pus (the Son) as the T etragrammation, is said to be ex tended in the form of a cross, thus-in Golgotha (the skull).

"And amid the insupportable brilliance of that mighty light, as it were, the likeness of a head appeareth. (That is! the highest crown is found in M acroprosopus) .

"And above him is the plenteous dew, diverse with two-fold color. (Like as in Macroprosopus it is white alone, so here it is white and red, on account of the judgments).

"It is written in Isa. XXXIII.20: 'Thine eyes shall behold Jerusalem at peace, even thy habitation.'

"The 'peaceful habitation' is the Ancient One, who is hidden and concealed.

"Macroprosopus is only the COMMENCEMENT OF THE MANIFESTED DEITY.

"And when a man wisheth to utter his prayers rightly before his Lord and his lips move themselves in this manner, his invocations, rising up-ward from him, for the purpose of magnifying the majesty of his Lord, *unto the place of abundance of pure* water *where the depth·of that foun-tain* riseth and floweth forth (that is under standing emanating from wisdom)) ; then (that fountain floweth forth plentifully, and) spreadeth abroad, so as *to* send down the influx from the Highest, downward from that place of abundance of water, *into paths singly and conjointly,* even unto the last path; in order that her bountiful grace may be derived into all from the highest downward."

27

SANTA CLAUS

All down the ages there have been stories of fairies, gnomes, mermaids, naiads and fabled characters galore. The ancient Norsemen, Dutch, Huns and all the oriental races, possess literature prolific with allegories, parables and fables built around the wonders and physical

and chemical operations of the human body.

The birth of the monthly seed is the basis of the Mother Goose Stories and similar tales in all lands.

Santa Claus, or Saint Nicholas, the patron saint of sea farers, virgins and children, is the bearer of gifts to chil dren on Christmas eve.

Of all festivals celebrated all over the known world, that held in honor of Santa Claus ranks as first in the hearts of all humanity, old as well as young. This in itself is a most significant fact. •

It is time that the truth in regard to this age long custom be made known to the world, time that its real and true significance be understood. Then will it be *truly* celebrated, for it will have become an inward process, as well as an outward observation.

Parents, from time immemorial, have explained to their children that the presents which they found in their stockings, when they jumped eagerly from their beds in the morning, were placed there by a mysterious person called "Santa Claus." No one saw him come, no one saw him leave, but he left unmistakable evidence of his visit.

Some children ask many questions in regard to this mysterious "person," and when they become too insistent the ingenuity of parents is sorely taxed to give satisfactory answers. There comes a time, however, when they must have the Santa Claus "myth" explained to them, and it is then that their deep childlike trust and confidence in their parents receives its first shock. Thereafter they com mence to doubt their parents, to question their veracity,

and many tears have been shed, because, after all Santa was not a "really, truly person."

THERE IS A SANTA CLAUS, IT IS A *PHYSIO LOGICAL* FACT, and IT does "SECRETE" the most holy and wonderful "gift" or *substance* in the body of every individual. Those who understand it-who receive it in the right spirit-have "Become as little children."

"As above, so below." As in the Macrocosm-the universe, so in the microcosm-man.

Can anyone think for one momtnt that the parables, fables, allegories and myths that have come down to us through the ages have no basic foundation?   They, as well as the fast days and feast days are founded on great esoteric truths. Otherwise they would have ceased to be.

The Great Hierarchy that rules the Universe see to it that nothing is forgotten that *needs* to be remembered. Santa Claus, or Saint Claus, is derived from the same root word as "claustrum," from which "cloister" is also derived.   Claustrum means a barrier, a covered place, se clusion. Cloister is referred *to* as a place of seclusion, and more especially as a place of seclusion for something

holy, something dedicated *to* divinity.

There is a Saint Claus, or Claustrum within the cere brum, and whoever gave it that name *knew why* they did so.

The suture of the skull is the point where the bones meet. We can very easily see this place on the head of infants, as the sections are not then drawn closely *to* gether, and the vibrations of the brain can be both seen and felt.

In Sanscrit this is called "The Door of Brahm," for it is the apperture through which the Ego, or Spirit leaves the body. It is also the chim:ney of Santa Claus.

The vertebrae as a whole is called the "stick of Brahm."

Directly underneath the "door of Brahm" is a tri angular shaped body named in physiology the "Island of Reil." This is the place where "John" was when "he" looked back and saw the wonderful vision of the regen erated man in the *"Isle* of Patmos" This island is the central lobe of the cerebrum, and is also called the *Pole;*

hence, the Island of Reil is the North Pole of the body, and is, as we well know, the *imperishable, sacred land.* In Santee's anatomy of the brain and spinal cord, we find that this island is "situated in the medial wall of the lateral fissure of the cerebrum, between the frontal, parietal and temporal lobes, whose growth, after the fifth month in utero, gradually covers it over.   At the end of the first year of extrauterine life, it is entirely concealed by temporal, parietal and frontal parts of the operculum"

-cover or lid. Thus we see that Mother Nature has taken great pains to conceal this sacred center.

Underneath this island, and directly in a line with the Optic Thalamus lies the Claustrum, but separated from it by yet three other bodies.

The claustrum is thin sheet of isolated gray matter, found just medial to the Island of Reil. Santee says it "is a sheet of peculiar gray substance, and is made up of fusiform (spindle shaped) cell-bodies." It is from this claustrum that contains yellow substance within its outer grayish exterior, that the wonderful, priceless OIL is formed that flows down into the olivary fasciculus, "de scending with the rubro-spinal tract through the reticular formation in the pons and medulla to the lateral column of the spinal cord. It terminates in the gray matter of the spinal cord, probably giving off collaterals to cor responding nuclei in the brain *stem."-*

Santee. This is the OIL, the precious gift of which the Bible speaks, "Thou anointest my head with oil."

And not only is there oil manufactured within this

·special laboratory of the brain, but there is actually an *olive tree,* which bears actual olives-so named in any anatomy. The two olives are two infinitesimal eminences on either side of the medulla, with the Pyramid between. They are one-half inch in length. It is found well de veloped only in the higher mammals. They are RELAY (Santee) stations between the cerebrum and the cere beHum and between the spinal cord and the cerebellum.

This oil is the most sacred substance in the body-it is the quintessence of gold-the "Gold of Ophir"-most truly a rare gift. Globules of oil are found in the vital fluid, the semen, and when the prodigal son has wasted

his substance, he finds that it takes a long time to replace the deficiency and make good the looted bank account.

This wonderful oil is the secret work of the immaculate Virgin, Mary (or Mare) 'represented by the sign Virgo. In chemistry we find that sulphate of potassium is the mineral salt, which, uniting with sulphur and oxygen, manufactures the oil. We find that this salt also crystal lizes out from the mother-liquors of sea water and salt springs. People born under the sign Virgo, if they have become deficient in this salt suffer from dryness of the skin, and baldness. We can also understand why draining of the vital fluid-living in excesses, will also produce baldness. If there were no oil in the body, the skin would become harsh and dry.

The story of the wise virgins who had their lamps trimmed and filled with oil is given to emphasize the necessity for the presence of oil in the body, for they cannot go out to meet the "bridegroom" unless their lamps are burning. "The lamb is the *lamp* thereof."

The olives, which contain the oil, are the reservoirs the relay stations, of course, which furnish the oil for the lamp, the pineal gland, at the top of which is the flame or eye. When the Kundalini, the serpent fire that lies con cealed within the sacral plexus is awakened, burns up the dross within the spinal cord, and reaches the conarium, it sets fire to this oil and thus lights the "perpetual lamp," which "Gives the light to the whole house."

Santa Claus is thus the giver of the supreme gift in the human body, the oil.for the perpetual lamp-the gold of Ophir, the quintessence of richness..

A total lack of oil in the body will, in itself, cause death.

Santa Claus brings his gifts when the *Christ-mass* is celebrated.

The Greek characters that stand for Christ are X PI, and the word it-self (Christ) means oil, in Greek. The seed is the bread of life, and when anointed with oil (Christed and crucified) become the Christ-mass-the bread, eaten in the Father's Kingdom.

Thus we now clearly understand the meaning of Santa Claus and his Christmas visit with gifts to the children.

28

LEAP YEAR

L EVITICUS 19 :23, 24, 25: "And when ye shall come into the land, and shall have planted all man ner of trees for food, then ye shall count the fruit

t hereof as uncircumcised; three years shall it be as uncir cumcised unto you; *it* shall not be eaten of.

"But in the *fourth* year all the fruit thereof shall be holy to praise the Lord withal.

"And in the fifth year shall ye eat of the fruit thereof that it may yield unto you the increase thereof: I am the Lord, your God."

Deuteronomy 14 :22 to 24: "Thou shalt truly tithe all the increase of thy seed that the field bringeth forth year by year.

"And thou shalt eat before the Lord thy God, in the place which he shall choose to place his name there, the tithe of thy corn, of thy wine and of thine oil and the firstlings of thy flocks; that thou mayest learn to fear the Lord thy God always." •

We find that in one year there are twelve moons and a fraction equal to just about one-third. Therefore, it would require just three years to make an extra moon or month. This is where "Leap Year" comes in, as at that time there was great rejoicing, for at the end of three years all the tithes were gathered and laid up within the gates. This represents the seed of the field, one seed being saved every month, and at the end of the three years, if all seeds have been saved, there would be thirty six and, with the extra month added, would make a total of thirty-seven seeds. As seven represents or stands for the conqueror, we can easily see that there is some special significance in this 37th seed, and also a great significance to the fourth year. The seed born at this time must have some special function to perform in the physiological economy and must be the seed which begins to lay the

foundation of the temple. For the seeds that are saved for three years complete a certain process in the body (if all are saved during that time) ; so that, with the beginning of the fourth year a special and most wonderful process begins. It is probable that the thirty-six seeds have been carried into the blood and completed the cir cuit of the body, producing a very great change therein, so that, when the three year process is completed, the thirty-seventh seed, or conqueror, is born and is the cause of very great rejoicing, as then the results of the three years, the tithes, are "collected within the gates"-taken to the Holy of Holies and used to lay the foundation of that sacred place.

I Kings 7 :13 and 14: "And King Solomon sent and fetched Hiram out of Tyre.

"He was a widow's son of the tribe of Naphtali."

Naphtali refers to the Pisces sign and, of course, means fish. Therefore, Solomon used the fish, or seed born in the sign Pisces, to commence the building of his temple. As in Leap Year we add *one day* to February, making 29, we utilize this day or *man* (seed) for a special work, in the human body, every fourth year, in the Pisces month.

There are thirteen full moons every fourth year.

29

REVELATION OF HERMES

The Ne Plus Ultra Statement on Physical Regeneration," by Para celsus, written at a time and in an age when concealment of deep esoteric truths was made necessary because of persecution by its enemies. Para celsus has reserved the last line for the revealment as well as the con cealment of the /great key.

, 'THE Book of Revelation of Hermes, interpreted

)Y Theophrasyus Paracelsus, concerning the *Su f>reme Secret of the World.*"

"Hermes, Plato, Aristotle and other philosophers, flourishing at different times, who have introduced· the Arts, and more especially have explored the secrets of in ferior creation, all these have eagerly sought a means whereby man's body might be preserved from decay and become endued with immortality. That there is *one 1hing* which may postpone decay, renew youth and prolong short human life.

Therefore, the above philosophers and many others have sought this ONE THING with great labor and have found that which preserves the human body from corruption and prolongs life itself, with respect to other elements, as it were like the heavens; from which they understood that the heavens are a substance above the Four Elements. And just as the heavens with respect to the other elements are held to be the fifth substance (for they are indestructible, stable, and suffer no foreign ad mixture), so also this ONE THING (compared to the forces of our body) is an indestructible *essence,* drying up all the superfluities of our bodies, and has been philosoph ically called by the above mentioned name. It is neither hot and dry like fire, nor cold and moist like water, nor warm and moist like air, nor dry and cold like earth. But it is a *skillful, perfect equation* of all the *elements,* a *right commanding of natural forces,* a *most particular union of spiritual virtues* and an *indissoluble uniting of body and soul.* It is the purest and noblest *substance* of an inde-

S tructible body, which cannot be destroyed nor harmed by the elemients, and produced by art. With this Aristotle prepared an *apple* (Fruit-seed, Authors) prolonging life by its scent, when he, fifteen days before his death, could neither eat nor drink on account of his old age. This spiritual *Essence,* or ONE THING, was revealed from above to Adam (man), and was greatly desired by the Holy Fathers; this also Hermes and Aristotle call the truth without lies, the most sure of all things certain; the secret of all secrets. It is the last and highest thing to be sought under the heavens. (Nate by authors: "There is only ONE WAY *under heaven,* whereby ye may be saved-Jesus, Christed and crucified.")

"A wondrous closing and finish of philosophical *work,* by which are discovered the *dews of heaven* and the fast ness of earth. What the mouth of man cannot utter is all found in this spirit. As Morienus says: 'He who has this has all things and wants no other aid,' for in it are all temporal happiness, bodily health and earthly fortune. It is the spirit of the fifth substance, a *fount of all joys (beneath the rays of the Moon),* the supporter of Heaven and Earth, the mover of Sea and Wind, the outpourer of Rain, upholding the strength of all things and an excellent irit above heavenly and other spirits, giving Health, Joy, Peace, Love; driving away Hatred and Sorrow, bringing in Joy; expelling all Evil, quickly *healing all dis eases,* destroying poverty and misery, leading to all good things, preventing all evil words and thoughts; giving man his *heart's desire* ('Seek ye first the Kingdom of God and His righteousness and *all things* shall be added unto *you'-Bible),* bringing to the pious, earthly honor and long life, but to the wicked who *misuse it,* eternal punish ment.

"This is the Spirit of Truth, which the world cannot comprehend without the interposition of the *Holy Ghost,* or without the instruction of those who knew it. The same is of a *mysterious nature, wondrous streng_!h and boundless power.* The saints from the beginning of the world have desired to behold its face for it heals all *dead* and living bodies.

H ere *Christ ism witness* that I lie not, for all heavenly influences are united and combined therein. This essence also reveals all treasures in earth and sea, converts all metallic bodies into gold, and there is nothing like unto it under heaven. This Spirit is the secret, hidden from the beginning, yet granted by God to a few holy men for the revealing of these riches to His glory-dwelling in fiery form in the air, and leading earth with itself to heaven, while from its body there flows whole rivers of living water./ This Spirit flies through the midst of the heavens like a morning mist, leads its burning fire into the water and has its shining realm in the heavens. And although" these writings may be regarded as false by the reader, yet *to the initiated* they are true and possible, when the *hidden sense* is properly understood. For God is wonderful in His works and His wisdom is without end. This Spirit in its fiery form is called a Sandaraca, in the aerial a Kybrick, in the watery an Azoth, in the earthly Alcohouh and Aliocosoph. Hence they are de ceived by these names, who, without instruction, think to find this Spirit of Life in things *foreign to our art.* For, although this Spirit which we seek, on account of its quali ties, is called by these names, yet the same is not in these bodies and cannot be in them. For a refined Spirit can not appear except in a body suitable to its nature. And, by however many names it may be called, let no one imagine that there be different spirits, for, say what one will, there is but one Spirit working everywhere and in all things. That is the spirit which, when rising, illumi nates the heavens, when setting incorporates the purity of earth, and when brooding has embraced the waters. This spirit is named Raphael, the Angel of God, the subtlest and purest, whom the others all obey as their king.

Through the same, Moses made the golden vessels in the Ark, and King Solomon did many beautiful works to the honor of God. Therewith Moses built the Taber nacle, Noah the Ark, Solomon the Temple. By this Ezra restored the Law and Miriam, Moses' sister, was *hos pitable.* Abraham, Isaac and Jacob and other righteous men have had life-long abundance and riches, and all the

S aints possessing it have therewith praised God. For it is the best of all things, because, of all things mortal that man can desire in this world, nothing can compare with it, and in it alone is truth. Hence it is called the STONE and Spirit of Truth; its praises cannot be sufficiently ex pressed.

0, unfathomable abyss of God's wisdom, which thus hath united and comprised in the virtue and power of One Spirit the qualities of all existing bodies. 0, unspeakable honor and boundless joy granted to mortal man; for the destructible things of nature are restored by virtue of said Spirit. 0, mystery of mysteries, most secret of all secret things, and healing and medicine of all things. Thou *last discovery* in earthly na tures, last best gift to Patriarchs and Sages, greatly desired by the whole world. 0, what a wondrous and laudable spirit is *purity* in which stand all joy, riches, *fruitfulness* of life, and art of all arts, a power, which to Initiates grants all material joys. 0, de sirable knowledge lovely above all things beneath the circle of the Moon, by which nature is strength ened, and heart and limbs are renewed, blooming youth is preserved, old age driven away, weakness destroyed, beauty and its perfection pre served and abundance insured in all things *to* men. 0, thou Spir itual *substance,* lovely above all things. 0, thou wondrous power, strengthening all the world. 0, thou invincible virtue, highest of all that is, although despised by the ignorant, yet held by the wise in great praise, honor and glory, that proceeding from humors' wakest the dead, ex pellest diseases and restorest the voice of the dying. 0, thou treasure of treasures, mystery of mysteries, .called by Avicenna "An unspeak able substance," the purest and most perfect soul of the world, than which is nothing more costly under heaven, unfathomable in nature and power, wonderful in virtue and works, having no equal among creatures, possessing the virtues of all bodies under heaven.   For from it flows the water of life, the OIL AND HONEY of *eternal healing,* and thus hath it nourished them with *honey and water from the rock.* Therefore, saith Morienus: "He who hath it the same hath all things."   Blessed art thou,

Lord God of our fathers, in that thou hast given the

P rophets this knowledge and understanding that they have hidden these things (lest they should be discovered by the blind and those drowned in worldly godlessness) by which the wise and the pious have praised thee.

"Oh, you doubtful man, you Peter of little faith, who are moved by each wind and sink easily. You are *your self* the cause of all your *diseases,* because your faith is so little and feeble, and *your own evil thoughts are your enemies.* Moreover, you have hidden within yourself a magnet which *attracts those influences which correspond to your will,* and this celestial magnet is of such power that for more than a hundred, or even thousands of miles, it attracts that which you desire out of the four elements."

Moral: Purify your desires. *Save the seed.*

"Matter and force are *one* and originate from the same cause."

"True knowledge consists in a direct *recognition* of TRUTH, and is taught by nature herself."

"The highest aspect of alchemy is the *regeneration* of man in the Spirit of God from the *material elements of his physical body.* The physical body *itself* is the greatest of mysteries, because in it are contained, in a condensed, solidified and corporeal state, the very essences which go to make up the substance of the material man, and this is the secret of the "Philosopher's Stone." The sign in which the true alchemist works is the *cross,* because man, standing erect among his brothers of the animal kingdom, roots with his material elements in the earth, penetrates with his soul through the elementary forces of nature to *suffer* and die, but his head reaches above the animal creation into the pure atmosphere of heaven."

"All the powers of the universe are potentially con tained in man, and man's physical body and all his organs are nothing else but products and representatives of the powers of nature. What is the human body but a con stellation of the same powers that formed the stars in the sky? He who knows what Iron is, knows the attributes of Mars. He who knows Mars, knows the qualities of iron. What would become of your heart if there were . no sun in the universe? To grasp the invisible elements, to attract them by their material correspondences, to con-

trol, purify and transform them by the *living power of the Spirit-this* is true alchemy."

"Faith is a luminous star that leads the honest seeker into the mysteries of nature. You must seek your point of gravity with God ('Seek ye first the Kingdom of God') and put your trust into an honest, divine, sincere, pure and strong *faith*, a,nd cling to it with your whole heart, soul, sense and thought, full of love and confidence. If you have such a faith, God will not withhold his Truth from you, but He will reveal His works to you, *credibly, visibly and consolingly.* This means that by the power of God acting within you and *opening your own* inner senses, God will reveal His works within yourself; so that His wisdom being born within, you may recognize through you, and you with it, the truth in all nature."

"Nature is the universal Mother of all and, if you are in harmony with her, if the mirror of your mind has not been made blind by the cobwebs of *speculations and mis conceptions and erroneous theories* she will hold up before you a mirror in which you will see the truth. But he who is *not true to himself will* not see the truth as it is taught by nature, and it is far easier to study a number of books and to *learn by heart* a number of *scientific theories* than to ennoble ones own character to such an extent as to *enter into perfect harmony* with *nature* and be able to *see* the *truth.*"

"Those living in vice are unworthy of it. Therefore is

this Art to be shown to all God-fearing persons, because it cannot be bought with a price. I testify before God that I lie not, although it appears impossible to fools that no one hath hitherto explored Nature so deeply. The Almighty be praised for having created this Art-the seed) and for revealing it to God-fearing men. Amen ! And thus is fulfilled this precious and excellent work, called the revealing of the Occult Spirit, in which be hidden the secrets and mysteries of the world. But this Spirit is one genius, one divine, wonderful and lordly power. For it embraces the whole world and overcomes the elements. *TO OUR TRISMEGISTUS SPA GYRUS, JESUS CHRIST, BE PRAISE AND GLORY IMMOR- TAL. AMEN!*"

30

EXTRACTS FROM THE SECRET DOCTRINE

B y Madam H. P. Blavatsky, the Greatest Occultist of the 20th Century

,'**SEED** OFLIFE, FISH: While Vaivasvata was engaged in devotion on the river bank, a FISH craves his protection from a *bigger fish*. He *saves*

it and places it in a jar (solar plexus) which, growing larger and larger, it communicates to him the news of the forthcoming deluge."

"Vaivasvata Manu, the *Son of Surya, the Sun* and Savior of our race, is connected with the *SEED OF LIFE,•* both *physically* and *spiritually.*"

"For them the passage entrance and the Sarcophagus in the King's Chamber meant *regeneration,* not *gener tion.* It was the most solemn symbol, a HOLY OF HOLIES, indeed, *wherein were created Immortal Hiero phants* and *Sons of God.*"

Page 63, Vol. III: " 'The first man is of the earth, earthy; the second (inner-our higher) man is the Lord from heaven * * * Behold, I show you a mystery.'

-*Bible.* Thus says Paul, mentioning the dual and trini tarian man for the better comprehension of the non initiated. But this is not all, for the Delphic injunction has to be fulfilled; man must know himself in order to become a perfect adept. How few can acquire the knowl edge, however, not merely in its inner, mystical, but even in its *literal sense,* for there are two meanings in this command of the Oracle. This is the doctrine of Buddha and the Bodhisattvas pure and simple."

SATAN: "Many names hath God given him (Satan), names of mystery, secret and terrible."

"The adversary, because matter opposeth Spirit, and time accuseth even the saints of the Lord."

"For Satan is the magistrate of the Justice of God (Karma). He beareth the balance and the sword."

"For to him are committed WEIGHT AND MEAS URE AND NUMBER."

Hades, or the Limbo of Illusion, of which theology makes a region bordering on hell, IS SIMPLY OUR GLOBE, the earth, and thus Satan is called "the angel of the manifested worlds."

It is Satan who is the God of our planet and the **ONLY** GOD, and this without any metaphorical illusion to its wickedness and depravity.   For *he is one with the Logos.* "The Gnostics wei;e right, then, in calling the Jewish God an 'Angel of Matter,' or he who breathed (con scious) life into Adam, and whose planet was Saturn. 'I create good and I create evil, I the Lord God create

all these things.' "-*Bible, Isaiah.*

"When the church, then, curses Satan, -it curses the Kos mic reflection of God. It anathematizes God made mani fest in Matter, or in the *objective;* it maledicts God, or the ever-incomprehensible Wisdom, revealing itself as Light and Shadow, Good and Evil in Nature, in the only manner comprehensible to the limited intellect of man."

"It was by Kriyashakti, that mysterious and divine power, *latent* in the *WILL* of every man, which *if not called to life,* QUICKENED AND DEVELOPED BY YOGA TRAINING, *remains dormant in 999,999 men out of a million,* and so gets *atrophied.*"

"It is this mysterious· POWER OF THOUGHT, which enables it to produce external, perceptible, *pheno menal* results by its own inherent energy. The ancients held that any idea will *manifest* itself *externally,* if one's attention and will is deeply concentrated upon it."

"Mystically Jesus was held to be man-woman."

"The ship or ARK-Navis-in short, being the sym bol of the female generative principle, is typified in the heavens by the moon and on earth by the womb; both being the vessels and bearers of the SEEDS of life and being, which the SUN, or Vishnu, the male principle (SON), vivifies and fructifies."

"Water is the symbol of the FEMALE ELEMENT everywhere: Mater, from which comes the letter 'M' is derived *pictorially* from MMM, a water hieroglyph."

"The human Ego is neither Atman nor Buddhi, but

the Higher Manas."

"MAN NOT CREATED FROM NOTHING: Very

soon the day will dawn, when the world will have to choose whether it will accept the miraculous creation of man (and Kosmos) out of NOTHING, according to the *dead* letter of Genesis, or a *first man* born from a fantastic link, *absolutely* 'missing,' so far-the common an-cestor of man, and of the 'true ape.'   *Between* these TWO FALLAC-IES, Occult philosophy steps in.   It teaches that the first human stock was projected by *higher and semi-divine* beings out of their *own essences.*"(See Prov erbs quoted elsewhere.)

"Man's (mankind) symbol is the cube unfolded and 6 becoming 7, or .the 3 crossways (the female) and 4 vertically; and this' is *man,* the culmination of the deity on earth, *whose body is the cross of flesh,* ON, THROUGH AND IN WHICH HE IS EVER CRU CIFYING AND PUTTING TO DEATH THE DI VINE LOGOS, HIS *HIGHER SELF.*"

"A few years longer and this system (numerical and geometrical keys) will kill out the dead-letter reading of the Bible, as it will that of all the other exoteric faiths, by showing the dogmas in their real naked meaning. And then this undeniable meaning, however incomplete, will unveil the mystery of Being, and will, moreover, entirely change the modern scientific systems of Anthropology, Ethnology and especially that of Chronology."

"The glyph of Pharaoh's daughter (woman) and the Nile (the great deep and water) and the baby boy found floating therein in the ark of rushes, was not primarily composed for, or even by Moses. It was anticipated in the fragments found on the Babylonian titles, in the story of King Sargon, who lived far earlier than Moses."

31

WHY REINCARNATE?

It is taken for granted that we, spiritual Egos, reincarnate for the sole purpose of obtaining knowledge that will enable us to triumph over matter.

If this statement is a true presentation of the great mystery of flesh and blood, it is indubitable evidence that we failed to obtain the wisdom that we are seeking in all the past incarnations and experience in flesh and blood.

Nowhere in sacred, or secret script, do we find a line indicating that any definite number of incarnations are required for spiritual man, or the "I AM" before the realization comes as expressed in the language of the allegorical Master, "I can lay my body down and I can take it up again," and again, "All the things that I do ye can do and greater things shall ye do." The time to do this great work is *now*. *"Now* is the accepted TIME. *Now* is the day of Salvation."

It is most encouraging to those who seek the Kingdom of the Real to find in the physiological and chemical writings of the Bible, that the process of attainment of this tremendous truth is so plainly set forth in both Old and New Testaments, that the "wayfaring man, though he be a fool," may understand.

There is but "One way whereby ye may be saved." Jesus, the monthly seed, christened in the waters of

Jordan, the marrow or oil of the spinal cord, and crucified (refined or *transmuted)* by *crossing* the nerves of regener ation at the junction of the medulla and cerebellum at the base of the skull, Golgotha, where the christened or christed seed is crucified, or crossified, in the regenerative process.

Matthew 19th Chapter: "Ye which have followed me *in* the regeneration, when the Son of man shall sit *in* the throne of his glory, ye also shall sit upon twelve thrones judging the Twelve Tribes of Israel." Son of man refers

to the seed, of which there are twelve and one-third born yearly, here represented by the Twelve Disciples of Jesus. Israel also means the seeds "Warriors of God" and the twelve thrones are typical of the twelve bodily functions

mastered by the regenerated seeds.

"The Kingdom of Heaven," "The Temple of God," "Work out your own salvation," and the multiple epi grams of sacred symbolism are no longer meaningless phrases to be mouthed, parrot-like, but they are coming to be realized as the thunder-lipped speech from the Infinite One.

Out of the chemicalizing mass of God's creative com pounds,..w.-e may see outlines of a new life, a new heaven and a new earth traced on the murky background of grime and dust and,battle smoke.

Earth's catyclism, the world war, has rent the veil of illusion, and many have come forth from the grave, and with the *eye* behind the *eyes* behold the "Real."

Within the "Temple, not made with hands," there dwells the spiritual Ego-a Son of the living God, preach ing in the wilderness of doubt and error, "Now is the accepted time, now is the day of salvation and now the Kinrrdom of Heaven is at hand."

"There is a spirit in man *and* the wisdom of the Almighty giveth it understanding."

32

THE LAKE OF HELL-FIRE AND BRIMSTONE

THE lower portion of the torso, bowels, etc., is called "hell," a "grave or lake," many times in the Scrip tures. Sulphur is a product of brimstone.   There is more or less sulphur in all foodstuffs. Over eating results in an over supply of sulphur, *i. e.,* brim-stone.   Over eat ing causes acidity. A portion of the food, failing to di gest, ferments, and acid results.   The acid, uniting with sulphur causes heat, fire, fever; hence hell, fire and brim

stone are chemical statements.

The vital force, or fluids of the body, is the Soul that is injured, devi-talized, destroyed in the poisons of the intestinal tract called Egypt and Sodom.

Thus can a man lose his soul in hell, fire and brim stone, *here* and *now.*

But, "As by man came death into the world, so by man came also the resurrection of the dead," *seed.•*

"Let the wicked man forsake his ways" (cease to eat of the fruit of the tree of life) , "and return unto the Lord who will abundantly pardon," and thus save his soul. All who bodily die lose their soul, for, says Job, "As the soul of a beast goeth downward, at death, so doth the soul of man."

Certainly, for "The wages of sin (ignorance) is death."

But the soul is not the spiritual Ego, and man is *body, soul and spirit*. When the "spirit in man" receives the "wisdom of the Almighty" and understands, it is then able to lift up and transmute the soul fluids and disinte grate both fluid and flesh, as the ascension of the seed Jesus, or Elisha, or Enoch are made to show, in the fables and parables.

"All that I do ye may do."

33

PHYSICAL REGENERATION

T HE inner eye-"the eye behind the eye"-just above and attached to the pineal gland by delicate electric wires, or nerves, is called Optic Thalamus, and

m eans "Ligh't, or Eye of the chamber."
     In the Greek, it means "The light of the World." "The Candlestick," "Wise Virgins," "The Temple Needs no light of the Sun," "If thine eyes be Single, Thy Whole Body shall be Full of Light," and other texts in the New Testament' refer to the single eye or Optic.

Let us now search for the oil that feeds this wonderful lamp, the All-Seeing Eye.

Christ Jesus is made to say "I Am the Light of the World." The word "world" comes from "whirl," to turn as a wheel, to gyrate, etc.

The human body is a certain rate of activity, motion or whirl, *i. e.,* world, and light of the world and the temple that needs no light of sun or moon refer to the body "Temple of God," when there is "oil in the lamp."

Error is not sanctified by age. It behooves every lover of truth to cast aside prejudice and dogma and find truth. Until we know the meaning of the words "Jesus" and

"Christ" we will not understand the Bible which was written in Greek and Hebrew and translated and retrans lated all down through the centuries.

Constantine was told by the priests of his time that there was no forgiveness of crimes like those he was guilty of and so this Roman

Emperor devised the elan of salvation in order that the blood of the innocent Jesus (or Christ) might save him from eternal damna tion. An easy way out for this monster, and all the other blood-smeared tyrants, Kings, Emperors and Napoleons of finance, competition and war, from Pharaoh to the present-day rulers.

The word Jesus is from Ichthos, Greek for fish. The word "Christ" means a substance of oil consistency, an ointment or smear. Varnish or paints are used to pre serve or *save* wood or paper or cloth-hence they become Saviors.

At about the age of twelve, Jesus was found in the temple arguing with the doctors or teachers. The word "doctor" is from Latin "docere," to teach.

Every month in the life of every man or woman, after puberty, when the moon is in the sign that the sun was in at the birth of the individual, there is a psycho-physical seed or "Son of Man" born in the Solar Plexus or the pneumo-gastric plexus which in the ancient text was called the "House of Bread."

Bethlehem, from Beth, a house, and lehem, bread. "Cast thy bread upon the waters and it shall return to thee after many days." Waters are the blood and nerve fluids of the body that carries the fish on its "Divine Jour ney" to regenerate, save and redeem man. Nazareth means to cook. Nazarene means cooked. Cook means to prepare. Any materialized thing is bread, Nazareth, mass, maso, or dough. Thus the Catholic Mass. Also Mas-on. It will now be made plain why the Masons and Catholics are not in agreement, for our letter N is an abbreviation of the 14th letter of the Hebrew alphabet, Nun, a fish. By addnig N to Maso, the riddle of cooked or prepared fish was made so plain that the priesthood strenuously objected, and thus developed friction between the church and Masonry.

The disciples were fishermen.   The early Christians used a fish as their secret symbol.   Money to pay taxes was taken from the mouth of a fish. Bread and fish were increased until twelve baskets full were left, etc.   God prepared a fish to swallow Jonah. Jonah means dove. Dove means peace-the germ descending from the gray matter of the brain (see baptism of John).   The storm means sex desire.   The life seed was thus saved. "He that is born of God cannot sin (or fall short of knowl edge) for his seed (fish) remaineth in him."-*John*. The age of puberty is about twelve. Up to that age, a child

does not understand moral responsibility. "The first born" means the first seed or fish. Pharaoh, sex desire always tries to destroy the first born.

Before we explain the baptism in Jordan and the chris tening and the crucifixion, etc., let us briefly explain Moses, Joshua, Nile, Pharaoh and the children of Israel.

Egypt means the dark lower part of the body. That part of the body below the Solar Plexus is Egypt, or the Kingdom of Earth. All above the center constitutes the Kingdom of 'Heaven. ("The Kingdom of Heaven is within you.") The Manger, or Bethlehem, is the cen ter, or the balance.

Nile, Moses and Pharaoh's daughter, all refer to gen eration. (See overflow of Nile). It rises in the moun tains of the moon. Moses means "drawn from the water." Fish are drawn from water. "There are *two* fishes in our sea"-Vaughn. See Sign of Pisces, two fishes.

"Joshua the Son of Nun." Nun is Hebrew for fish. Moses was the physical or *generative* fish.

Moses' laws were on the *physical* plane.

Joshua means "God of Salvation," and salvation comes from saliva or *salivation*. Sal is salt which *Saves*. "If the salt loses its Savor" *i. e.* Savior, wherewith shall it be salted?" Saliva *saves* the body by digesting (or pre paring) the food. Saliva is a smear or ointment, and so Joshua compares with Christ as Moses compares with Jesus. Moses died on Mt. Nebo. Nebo means under standing. Joshua took the place left vacant by the death of Moses. Jesus was haptized *of* John in Jordan-the fluids, Christ-substance of the spinal cord and became "my beloved Son in whom I am well pleased." The word "John" IO H N NE S means "Soul" or "fluids of the body" and not the Ego or Spiritual Man. So when the body dies, the fluids die-thus man loses his soul when he loses his body. To prevent the loss of soul and flesh is the mission of the Son, or Seed, of God, or the Son of man.

But the question will be asked-what or where is the

Source or origin of this seed or redeeming Son? We answer: "Ether, Spirit or God."

Esse, Universal intelligence, or *It* may be used.   *It* breathes into man the breath of life. This elixir is carried through lungs into arteries, or air carriers, where it unites with the inorganic cell-salts, materializes (cooked) and forms granules, and is then deposited as flesh and bone. The study of Astrology, Biology and Biochemistry, added to Physiology, will lead one into the great Alchem ical laboratory of the "Fearfully and wonderfully made" human temple-the temple made without sound of saw

or hammer.

Before the Neophyte can fully realize the power of the Divine Eye within his own brain, he must understand the meaning of *Or* especially in its relation to *Word* and *Jordan*.

Or is gold, not metal, but the "precious substance" the seed. Dan is Hebrew for Judge, therefore the Crea tive Power operating through the precious substance pro duces Judgment, the man of good judgment or wisdom.

The upper brain is the reservoir of this *Or* and is the gray matter or "Precious Ointment" or Christ.

"In the beginning was the *Word* and the *Word was* God. *All things* were (or is) created by it" etc., etc.

The "Lost Word" is a symbol of the generative or animal thought eating the fruit of the Tree of Life thus destroying or losing the gold, "or," of the body.

Hiram means "high born," or the seed destined to reach the pineal gland and "Single Eye."

Tyre means a rock. By the conservation and trans mutation of the sex substance the pineal gland becomes firm and hard and is, in the fable, called rock (Tyre). "The wise man built his house, Beth or body, upon a rock." So here we have the explanation of Hiram Abiff. Abiff is derived from the word Abid-month.

Hiram Abiff (there are some who will understand) was resurrected during the delay caused by searching for his body: in other words a *month* passed and another seed was born which the candidate for initiation is ad monished *not to slay*.

The upper brain furnishes *all* that man contains, or is. Jesus was not a Savior until he was *Christed of John* in the *Jordan*. Then he became the "Beloved Son."

Why was the baptism necessary? Because there are two fish, one was Jesus the Carpenter, the man. The other, the *Christed* Jesus, the Son of God. The Christ substance gave the electric or magnetic power to the seed to cross the nerves at Galgotha without disintegrating or dying. *I*

To crucify, means to add to or increase a thousand fold. When electric wires are crossed, they set on fire all inflammable substances near them. When the Christed seed crossed the nerve at Galgotha, the vail of the temple was rent and there ,was an earthquake, and the dead came forth, *i. e.,* the generative cells of the body were quick ened or regenerated.

The crucifi xion or crossing of the life-seed gives power to vibrate the pineal gland at a rate that causes the "light of the chamber" to fill the "whole body with light" and send its vibration out along the optic nerve to the physical eye and thus heal the blind.

34

THIRTEEN, THE OPERATION OF WISDOM

T HE number thirteen is unlucky for ignorance only.

All so-called laws of nature may be reduced to thirteen.

The origin of words and their application vary widely. Thus the origin of twelve is circle or completeness, or without break or sin; that is complete. All operations that produce something may be called twelve, being com plete in order to produce, the product is therefore thir teen. Thus all machines or factories symbol twelve and the product thirteen.

THE ZODIAC

There are twelve constellations, the central suns of which constitute the signs of the Zodiac.

One sign rises every two hours, or so appears to our sense, because the rotation of earth causes the phenom enon, and the earth, or sun, makes thirteen.

THE HUMAN BODY

There are twelve functions of the human body and the seed, or psycho-physical germ, born in the solar plexus every 29¾ days. So then there are twelve moons and a fraction in *365* days. The pneumo gastric nr.rve, vagus nerve, that comes down from cerebellum across (a cross) the medulla oblongata branches out at the lungs (pneumo) and at the stomach (gastric), and is called "The Tree of Life" (thirteen letters), also pneumo gastric (thirteen letters).

There are twelve mineral salts in the blood and blood
. itself-the product-thirteen.

DAVID'S THIRTEEN SONS

1st Chr., 14th ch., 3d ver. "And David took more wives and concubines at Jerusalem; and David begat more sons and daughters."

H ere follows the names of thirteen children.

THIRTEEN CHILDREN OF JACOB

The 29th and 30th chapters of Genesis record the birth of eleven sons and one daughter, Dinah. The 35th chap ter records the birth of Benjamin, the 12th son and 13th child.

Jacob, in Hebrew, is circle, or to follow after, also represented in Hebrew symbology by a circle of men, each one with h'and holding the heel of the one in front, and thus describing a circle.

The origin of the allegory is founded in the rotation of earth and the apparent rising of one of the Signs of the Zodiac every two hours, making twelve, and the earth itself thirteen. •

The esoteric meaning is based in the marvelous oper ation of the wonderfully made human body. All of the parables, fables or allegories of the human organism are related to 13.

Moses, Joshua, Jesus, Christ and all the characters of the Scriptures are symbols of the psycho-physical seed that is born in, or *out_* of the solar "manger" in the center of the body.

Twelve symbols a circle, in Hebrew, meaning complete. The product of twelve is thirteen. Galilee is a circle. The Sea of Galilee, circle of water, or fluid, hence circulation of the blood and fluids of the body. So Jacob may be applied to the body.

Rachel means Ewe, or Mary, Eve or the manger (solar plexus) where Mary and Jesus were found. There is no U in the Hebrew alphabet, hence no double U.   So Vis the letter, or double V-hence EVE or *EVVE-i. e.,* Rachel. The solar plexus is symboled by many names in the Bible, all female, whether they refer to a man or a woman, because it gives birth to the seed.   This won drous redeeming seed is exactly the same in male and female and plays no part in generation, but is the "Plan of Salvation" whereby the child "born in sin" may be redeemed and saved. Thus, "In my Kingdom (regenera tion) there is no marrying," etc.

For key to Benjamin, the entire chapter, Genesis 35th, should be studied carefully in the light of the new reve lations.

Sixth verse, 35th chapter: "So Jacob came to Luz, the same is Bethel" (or Beth-lehem), house of bread, the solar plexus. "He built there an al- tar (same as "man ger" or plexus,-womb) and called the place "El-beth el," (God's house of God) because there God was re vealed, etc.

Sixteenth verse: "And they journeyed from Bethel and there was some distance to come to Eprath" (fruit, posterity, Bethlehem, seed).

Here Rachael "had hard labor" and gave birth to Ben oni and died. Ben-oni means "child of my sorrow," but Jacob called him Ben-Ja-min, "Son of my right hand."

Sixteenth to twentieth verse: "And Rachael died and was buried in the way to Ephrath (the same *is* Bethle hem). "And Jacob set up a pillar upon her grave; "The same is the pillar of Rachael's grave unto this day." The solar plexus, chamber or manger is the pillar.

The death of Rachael, the mother, simply means that thirteen com- pletes the number of seeds born during the thirteen moon months. See chapter on The Passover.

Great latitude must be given to writers of parables, fables and alle- gories.

Genesis, 35th chapter, 10th vers:!: "And God said unto him, thy name is Jacob (the circle), thy name shall not be called any more Jacob, but Israel shall be thy name."

Israel here clearly points to the seeds, thirteen, one every moon, that cross Jordan. Twelfth verse, 35th chapter: "And to thy seed after thee will I give the land."

Jacob (circle) means complete operation; and thirteen the seed, Is- rael, the product.

JOSHUA AND JERICHO

In the book of Joshua (Son of Nun), a fish-born in the solar plexus twelve times in *365* days and a fraction, see Leap Year, it is recorded that the host marched

a round the walls of Jericho once daily for six days and seven times on the seventh-thirteen.

Jericho, captured by the British troops, 1917, is situ ated thirteen miles outside the walls of Jerusalem.

JESUS AND THE TWELVE DISCIPLES

Before the crucifixion of Jesus, the seed, fish, there were twelve Disciples or workers and Jesus was the thir teenth. After the crucifixion, which means to *increase in power,* (note the increase in power of the electric current when the wires are crossed), Paul was added to the twelve Apostles. Paul is made to say: "I was born out of time."

The meaning of Paul is small or the "still small voice," as P is from the--Hebrew letter Pe, to speak, or the mouth. S is from the 21st letter of the Hebrew alphabet, Schin, meaning falling short of completeness as there are 22 letters in the Hebrew alphabet. So the allegory makes the allegorical character Saul before conversion, or re generation, and Paul, the *preacher,* after the transmuta tion.

There are no dates to the so-called Epistles of Paul. Neither are there dates to *any* of the writings-scrip tures-gathered by the Council of Nicara under the Pa gan Emperor, Constantine. No one knows when they were written.

THE UNITED STATES AND THIRTEEN

The thirteenth degree of the Zodiacal Sign Cancer was rising July 4th, 1776, when the Declaration of Independ ence was signed. Cancer represents the breast and is therefore the mother sign, or woman. M is from Mem, the thirteen letter of the Hebrew alphabet, and means *woman.* The United States plays the part of mother to all peoples and gathers them under her protecting care. We commenced our individuality as a nation with thirteen states.

In 1782 the obverse side of the United States Seal was made and contained thirteen stars, thirteen stripes, and an eagle with a quiver containing thirteen arrowheads in one talon and an olive branch with thirteen leaves in the other. And the motto "E pluribus unum" contains thirteen letters.

About this time, 1782, an unknown man appeared in Philadelphia and offered the drawing of a seal (see cut) which he suggested be added as the reverse side. This man declared that the seal would be adopted in the Year 1921, the digits of which equal thirteen, and that the eagle would no more be used.

Strange to say the stranger's seal was adopted, but has not come into prominence until within the past three or four years.

The reverse side of the United States Seal shows part of the pyramid of Egypt, the base of which covers thir teen acres.

There are thirteen steps or terraces. The motto over the pyramid, "Annuit Creptis," contains thirteen letters and is Latin for "Prosper us in our undertaking."

Our solar system has passed out of the water sign Pisces, and thus occurred the "end of the world"-thir teen letters.

So our great fleet of planets and flag ship Sun is now in the air or spiritual sign Aquarius.

In the allegory of the suns or sons of Jacob (see Gene sis 29), the fifth son born was Dan, a judge, thus Daniel

-"Judge appointed by God," as El is face of God in Hebrew.

The first son or sun was Reuben or Libra, the loins, therefore the fifth would be the legs, or Aquarius, sign of man, where the solar system is now and where it will remain for over 2000 years.

Day means an indefinite period of time-thus we say Napoleon's day or Lincoln's day. Therefore, t is plain to be seen that we are now in the "Day of Judgment," thirteen letters.

Woodrow Wilson---13 letters. He landed in France,

both trips to Europe, on the 13th. American soldiers crossed the Rhine the 13th. Gen. Pershing was born on the 13th.

The League of Nations is printed on thirteen pages. Every 4th year there are 13 moons.

Every year there are 12 moons and a fraction, thus

leap year-1,920, two new moons, July 1st and 30th.

35

DANIEL IN THE LIONS' DEN

THE word Dan, in Hebrew, means a judge. *Daniel,* judgment or God's judge. El or iel, in Hebrew, represents the supreme ruler or God. God and

good are synonymous, *i.e.* Daniel-good judgment or wisdom.

The word Darius, traced to its root, simply means an office, same as Presidency, and whoever fills the office is for the time called Darius.

Medes is from media, the middle, and is represented in the body by solar plexus.

Persia, the East, Persians, people of the East.

In scripture allegories East always means the back; West, the front; North-up, or the head; South, down the feet.

There is a wide difference between the original meaning of a word and the multiple applications of a word. For instance, lamb, dove, hog, wolf, eagle and names of all birds and animals represent ideas or principles that have been applied to different species of animal forms on the hypothesis that these names fitted some peculiar trait or habit of the animal or reptile to which they gave the appellation.

Lion means strength and is used to designate the "King of beasts" or animals. The part of the human body be low the solar plexus is referred to in the Scriptures (physiological writings) as Kingdom of Earth, hades, lower Egypt and the seat of sex desire (Pharaoh) or the animal passions, appetites, etc.

Ani: breath or soul.

Mal: bad, or imperfect, hence malformation, malnutri tion, bad breath or soul (unregenerated substance), or the *Animal* man.

The "Lion's Den" is used in the fable to typify the ani mal functions that were regenerated by wisdom or good judgment-Daniel.

The following definitions will assist the reader to more fully realize the esoteric meaning of words in scripture:

DANIEL-]udgment.

BELSHAZZAR-Bel, Belia! or Be-elzebub, has formed a king.

BELTSHAZZAR-A maintainer or Prince. (This title was given to Daniel after his regeneration as shown by the letter T from Tav, the 22nd letter of the Hebrew alphabet meaning cross, where the redeemer (seed) is crucified. "There is no name under heaven whereby ye may be saved except Jesus, the seed, *Christ-ed* and cruci fied."

NEBUCHADNEZZAR-From Nebo-understanding. A protector against misfortune.

ELAM-Unlimited duration.

A-BEDNEGO-Servant of Nego, *i.e.,* understanding. MESHACH-Guests of Sha, the Son-god.

SHADRACH-Royal or rejoicing in the way.

(Thus it is made clear why Shadrach, Meshach and A-bednego were not consumed in the fiery furnace. They are principles, eternal verities that are not affected by physical expressions and can, therefore, complete the ini tiation of the Ego.)

In the 8th chapter of Daniel, verses 1 and 2, we find the words "Shushan the palace which is in the province (or country) of Elam; and I was by the river Ulai."

ELAM-Eternity.

SHUSHAN-From Susanna, a lily (known as the Capi tol of Elam), real meaning, the product of divine mind.

ULAI-From Hebrew Pehlvi, meaning pure water.

Daniel was "By the river Ulai." Ulai here refers to the spinal cord. The marrow, or oil, in this channel is pure crystal in color.

"And he showed me a river of water of life, bright as crystal, proceeding out of the throne of God and the Lamb, in the midst of the street thereof. And on this side of the river and on that was the Tree of Life bearing twelve manner of fruits yielding its fruit every month; and the leaves of the tree were for the healing of the nations."

Month is from Moon (Moonth) and there are twelve and one-third moons in the Solar year.

Leaves are effects of a tree.

The monthly seed (fruit) when saved, not "eaten," heals disease and sin.

"Moses lifted up the serpent in the wilderness," the *body.*

Moses, the first born, the seed, desired to regenerate the blood and lead it to the promised land, thus he lifted up the animal•forces, sex desire, here symboled as the ser pent (see the temptation of Adam and Eve) ... So shall the "Son, or Seed, of Man be lifted up," etc., etc. that is put on the cross in order to reach the pineal gland. "If I be lifted up, I will draw all *men* unto me." I will draw all other seed unto me. Study the etymology of "men." Also read "The tree in the midst of the garden

bore fruit every month and its leaves were healing."

The Commandment to not *eat* of the *fruit* of this tree was not (is not) heeded by the race and death is the re sult.

The serpent said "Eat, thou shalt not die," but sex desire was a liar from the beginning.

A noted Professor of Greek in one of our universities

says that the translation of many New Testament texts from Greek are radically wrong. For instance, "He that saveth his life shall lose it, and he that loseth his life, for my sake, shall find it," should read: "He that saveth his seed-life-shall *loosen* it (set it free), and he that *loosens* it, shall find it," which means that this "Bread cast upon the waters" shall redeem him. Galilee means a circle of water-the fluids of the body.

Jesus walking on the water is a symbol of the seed, or fish, on its journey. Peter, from petra (stone) is a sym bol of physical or material thought which was rescued by the fish, Savior.

The Optic Thalamus, or light in the room, is called "The Lamb of God that taketh away the sins of the *world."* The Hebrew letters Lamed, Aleph, Mem and Beth form the word Lamb, meaning innocence or purity. Sin is from the Hebrew letter Schin, meaning to fall short of knowledge. Sin does not mean wrong or crime,

b ut one may commit a crime and do wrong through lack of knowledge. Paul said: "I die daily" . . . I am

- the chief of sinners." Revelation: "And the lamp thereof is the Lamb." The word "Lamb" ends with B, which means a house or body of some kind. Now, the optic or central single eye is a body, like the outer eye ball, therefore, a beth. This is called lamb by the ancient poet.

Lamp ending with P, which means speech or *sending forth* or radiating, is from Pe, the 17th letter of the He brew alphabet, and was used to express light or knowl edge emanating or going forth from this eye or "Lamb of God."

"As a man thinketh in his heart, so is he."

The cerebellum is heart-shaped, and in the Greek is known as the heart. The organ that divides blood was called the "Dividing Pump." The seat of thought is the Cerebellum. Our thoughts shape our lives. If we think continually below the solar plexus in the Kingdom of Earth; if we dwell in thoughts of material pleasures, we become animal and materialistic. If we really desire the Kingdom of Heaven, we must think of the process that will enable us to realize it.

When Jesus·was born, they put him in "swaddling clothes." Now the psychic germ (fish) is composed of the concentrated essence of life and is covered by a gos samer capsule for protection. If this swaddling cloth is broken, the "precious ointment" is lost, *i.e.* it disinte grates and corrupts the blood.

In order to save this germ of life, man must remember that as a man thinketh, so is he. While men must abstain

entirely from sexual contact, he must also realize that "He who looketh on a woman to lust after her, hath com mitted adultery with her in his *heart.*"

By constant prayer do we attain the Kingdom, for Jesus said "With man it is impossible; but with God all things are possible."

Envy, hatred, ambition, covetousness, will destroy the capsule that contains the seed and thus corrupt the blood, as surely as sexual contact. Alcohol in all its deceptive forms is the arch foe to this life-seed and seeks by every means known to the enemy of man to destroy it. "No drunkard shall inherit the Kingdom of Heaven" because alcohol destroys the redeeming substance that enables man to understand or think in his heart the thoughts of the Spirit. Alcohol cuts the capsule that holds the Esse born every month in Bethlehem. Alcohol eats the fruit of the tree of life.

Gluttony is another enemy to regeneration. All excess of food, all that is not burnt up in the furnace-the stom ach and intestinal tract, all that is not properly digested, ferments and ptoduces acid which develops alcohol.

Auto-intoxication is common among those who overeat.

Most everyone overeats.

The furnace, stomach and digestive tract becomes a distillery when the surplus food ferments, and thus be comes Babylon, the home of unclean birds and beasts which pander to carnal mind.   Here we have the reason why sickness was considered Sin by the ancients.

"To heal the sick and cast out devils" is the mission of the seed. "He that is born of God cannot sin, or be sick, for his seed remaineth in him." "The blood of Christ clean seth from all sin," therefore from all disease.   Here is the physiological explanation:

When the *Christed* sub stance, the ointment from the river of Jordan, the oil in the spinal cord, reaches the pineal gland, it vibrates to a rate that causes new blood-the *new wine.* This is the blood of Christ that heals all infirmities.   Unless so called Christians repent of their sins, the doom of the church is at hand, *"M ene, mene teckel upharsin"* is writ ten on the wall.

Here are the words that define a Christian: "These signs shall follow those who believe; they shall lay hands on the sick and they shall recover. They shall cast out devils and raise the dead. All the things that I do, ye shall do and greater things shall ye do."

If there be one Christian on earth today, let him stand forth and prove himself worthy. "He that overcometh, I will give to eat of the fruit of the tree of life." To overcome a habit is to *cease to do it.* When the earthly man is controlled by the spiritual man-the Lord God he ceases to eat of the fruit, th,it is, *waste it.* This fruit

• s then carried up to the brain and "Eaten in the Father's Kingdom." 1 "And the last enemy to be overcome is death." We *overcome* death by *ceasing* to die, and in no other way. "He that believeth in me, shall not perish." Those who die are sinners, and therefore are not Chris tians, for Christ Jesus was (is) without sin. "The wages of Sin is *death."* Repent, forsake evil, take up thy Cross, call upon the Lord and He will abundantly pardon. "And the ransomed of the Lord shall return and come to Zion." When the sexual functions are used for the propagation of human bodies, there is no condemnation or sin. Moth erhood is holy, pure, divine. But motherhood forced is crime. Unwilling motherhood has created the spirit of war and murder and well-nigh destroyed the race. Sexual union for pleasure alone is the broad road that leads to death. "And there shall be no more *Curse"-Revela* tion. The word "Curse" has no reference to an oath. Curse means friction, to grind. The statement "Then Peter began to curse and swear" . . . And immedi ately the cock crew," when understood physiologically, fully explains the meaning of curse. Sexual commerce for the birth of children where the parents sacrifice them selves for their offspring's sake, or total absti- nence, is written with a pen of flame on all the pages of ancient Scrip- tures and modern biology.

"And I saw a woman clothed with the Sun, having the Moon under her feet and twelve stars upon her head." The Sun is the Seed, the "Son of Man," the product of her own body, saved and lifted up. The Moon refers to the generative life. Twelve stars are the twelve func tions, typi- fied by twelve zodiacal signs, which she has mas tered through physical regeneration.

"When thou prayest, enter into thy closet and pray to thy Father in secret, and he shall reward thee openly."

The word Secret is derived from Secretions. The upper brain, the Cerebrum, contains the secretions, gray matter, creative or that which creates, builds and supplies *all* the life force of the human temple,-Soul of Man's (Solomon's temple). Hence God, the Creator, dwells in you. The cerebellum is his throne. Prayer or desires expressed by man in the cerebellum for righteousness is

answered in the cerebrum. Thus by prayer to God within, and in no other way, can man overcome the ad versary or the "carnal mind .which is at enmity to God."

All so-called sex reform that tolerates union of sexes, may be an- swered by:

"There is a way that Seemeth right to man,

The end of which is death."

"In my Kingdom there is no marrying nor giving in marriage, But they are as the

Angels in Heaven."

No page of the wonders of the human body-the tem ple of the, living God-is more divinely scientific than the parable that follows:

"The foolish man built his house on the sand And the rain washed,it away."

"The wise man built his house on a rock

And it stood the storms, for it was builded upon a rock."

The Bible is a compilation of astronomical, physiolog ical and anatomical symbols, allegories and parables.

In the technical terms of modern chemistry and physi ology the above text is explained as follows: Sand and cement form rock or stone. Sand alone, without some medium-cement-is unstable, simply "shifting sand."

The Pineal gland, the *dynamo* that runs the organism of man, is composed of sand plus a cement, an ointment, a smear, found, as has been explained, in the spinal cord, also to some extent, in all parts of the body. When this cement is wasted, as the Prodigal Son wasted his sub stance in riotous living, there being a deficiency of this precious oil, the pineal gland becomes pasty, and does not vibrate at a rate that vitalizes the blood and tissue at the health and strength rate, and the house, beth or body, falls.   •

In the common slang of the hour, we say: "He lacks the sand," or "grit."

The mineral salts of blood were called sand or salt by the Greeks. The cell-salts that are found in the pineal gland are chiefly potassium phos-phate, the base of the gray matter of the brain, and lime, but all of the 12 inor ganic salts are represented. In Revelation, the pineal

gland is called "the white stone." In Biochemistry, the phosphate of potassium is given as the birth salt of Aries people.

Those who build their house upon a rock are they who conserve the substance that unites with the sand-cell salts-and thus form the rock upon which a body may be built that will be free from sin and sickness.

The mission of Jesus, the Christ, was to *triumph over death* and the grave, over matter, and transmute his body and also materialize at will. He not only succeeded in doing this, but stated most emphatically that all the things that he did, we may do also.

Did he proclaim the truth? Answer, thou of little faith!

"Rock of Ages, cleft for me, Let me hide myself in thee."

36

NOAH, THE ARK AND THE ANIMALS

F EW theologians are there, of to-day, who insist on a literal interpretation of the biblical story of the flood, Noah and the ark.

T here are known to be 1656 species of mammals; 6266 species of birds; 642 of reptiles; 20 of oxen; 27 species of goats; 48 species of antelopes; insects, fish, turtles and creeping things on land and sea innumerable.

There is not a bit of geological evidence that the earth was ever totally sub"rnerged. But, going to the root of the words Noah, ark, Ararat, etc., it is quite easy to read the riddle of the allegory.

Noah is Hebrew for rest. Ararat simply means a mount or elevation. In English we say hill, mound, peak, mountain, etc. So in both Greek and Hebrew we find Nebo, Pisgah, Ararat, pinnacle of the temple, Zion, Gib eon, used to typify brain and pineal gland.

Ark, or boat, is used to symbol the seed (fish or Moses) born in the solar-plexus to be carried 1.,1p through the regenerative process to the pineal gland. Moses was found in an ark and the ark of the covenant was carried by the children of Israel (see Jacob's 13 children) through the wilderness and *across* Jordan, where the "waters stood up at the City of Adam."

Adam means earth or sand. At the source of the spinal cord there is a body called medulla oblongata. Medulla means marrow or thick oil or ointment. This oblong body (oblongata in Latin) is a bed of mineral salts of the body and marrow. This precious oil (Christ) is received there by secretions from the cerebrum, the upper brain-the "Most High."

This oil flows down the spinal cord to the Caudia Equina, and this is a symbol of the Jordan and Dead Sea of Palestine.

Jordan means the "Descender" or oil flowing down.

Witness: *Dove* or dive-to descend. Dove, *i.e.,* a diver
-"The Spirit of God descended like a dove, and a voice said, 'This is my Son,' " etc.

This occurred *af Jer* the baptism of Jesus, the seed, in Jordan, the oil or Christ.

The animals taken up to Ararat, the pineal gland, or "Pinnacle of the temple," simply means the transmutation of animal desires and propensities by saving the ark (seed) and crucifying it at Golgotha where it *Crosses* Jordan in medulla, the "Place of the Skull."

Woman the 4th Dimension.

The solar system has entered the "Sign of the Son of Man,"where it will remain for over 2000 years. In as trology this sign is symboled as "The Water Bearer," while in Bible Alchemy it is represented by Dan, the fifth son of Jacob, and means "judgment,11 or "he that judges."

From these statements it is easy to realize that all that is taking place in the world to-day is but a "working out" or a summing up of all that has been taking place for cen turies.

The world is awakening, the old order is passing, worn-out traditions that are no longer applicable to pres ent conditions must be replaced by new.

Radical and fundamental changes stare us in the face on all sides. Science, philosophy, religion, bodies politic and social-all are being shaken from their very founda tions-to be rebuilt anew.

There is no equilibrium, no balance, no harmony, no equality, anywhere.

Nowhere do we see a better illustration of this unbal anced condition of the world than in man's attitude toward woman. For some time, now, this viewpoint has been gradually changing and Aquarian vibrations, or, in other words, the vibratory influence of the planets, have made conditions possible for this change.

Woman is at last coming into her own.

Co-equal with man I Mighty strides toward the regen eration of the human race will now be made.

With equilibrium of forces now possible world har mony shall grow apace.

All these truths can be mathematically expressed.

F our (4) means realization-one and three (1 plus 3) equals four. Woman or mother comes from the Hebrew word Mem-M (womb, man, water, Mary-same meaning in all).

"I saw a woman clothed with the *Son,* the moon (from month-menses) under her *flfet.* She controlled the twelve functions of the body. The Son signifies "Sun" or "Son of Man," the seed or product of her own life, saved and lifted up. The Moon refers to the generative life. Twelve stars are the twelve functions, typified by the twelve zodiacal signs which she has mastered through physical regenera-tion.   •

Having been upon the cross, or having crossed over, the seed is Christed; and in the man or woman seeking to regenerate or "save," the seed is *saved,* it then enters the Optic Thalamus, the eye of the cham-ber, which "giveth light to all that are in the house," that is, to the twelve functions that are in the body, represented by the twelve signs of the zo-diac.

Woman regenerated-"clothed with the Sun"-is the Queen of Sheba, in Bible symbology, and is represented by the number seven (7).

Then woman is Queen of 7. Sheba is seven in He brew, and Solomon's temple (soul-of-man) is the physical body where the Queen of Sheba found so many wonders.

Queen of seven *what?*

Man is only three (3) dimensions. Dimension means *line.*

The human body as well as the universe are geomet rical figures, a fact which the old philosophers well knew, for they said that sound and number governed the laws of creation.

Man is proved to be a three dimensional creature by physiology; and woman is the fourth dimension, by the same means of proof.

In the thirty-first chapter of Jeremiah, twenty-second verse, we read: "A woman shall compass a man."

Mathematically, a woman can encompass a man.

Man cannot compass a woman, for he is only a three

line creature, while she is four. Therefore, four is able to compass, or contain within its radius, three.

Woman may be represented by the square (four lines). Man may be represented by the triangle (three lines). Three and four do not balance, and never have. There has not been universal harmony or balance between them, for man has never considered woman his equal until very recently.

But man is "coming off his high horse," and the scales will soon balance.

All down the ages man has considered himself the "lord of all creation." The "spare rib" which he so con descendingly parted with in the so-called "beginning" un balanced him entirely. He considered himself superior to woman and has continued to do so to the "end of the world," or "whorl of activity"-the activity or manifestation of the solar system in the last or previous sign, that representing the water age.

During the water age man conquered the water-inventions pertaining to water were perfected, etc., etc.

To return to the mathematical equation of man and woman:

The three dimensions or lines of man that can be shown on a physiological chart are the creative centers of the brain, the solar plexus and the sex organs . Woman also possesses the creative centers of brain, solar plexus and sex organs; *but* she also possesses another, and in a way the most wonderful of all-the *breast* that nourishes infant man. This is the fourth dimension or line. These imaginary lines are at equal distances from each other.

Work this out for yourselves on the chart and you will never forget it.

In the triangle drawn to represent man we find the eye, also. This is a well-known Masonic symbol.

See "The *Rib-lah* that made the *Wom(b)an.*"

37

TRANSLATIONS OF SCRIPTURE

"He that saveth his life shall lose it."-Mark 8 :35.

THE above sentence does not ring true and is not logical.

A Greek professor recently went to Oxford, England, for the sole purpose of looking into the Greek text in regard to this seeming inconsistency. (Also Luke 16:9. See below.)

The discovery was made that the letter N (from nun, mean-ing a fish), was omitted, also the letter 0, and that a correct translation reads: "He that saveth_his life shall *loosen* it," etc.

The seed, in the fable, or Jesus, said: "I am the way, the truth and the *!if e,"* etc. Therefore, he that saveth his life (Seed) shall loosen it so that it may enter the "Strait and narrow way," etc. This strait is the Spinal Cord. As has already been written, "I am the bread of life." Again, "Cast thy bread upon the waters"-i. *e.,*

the strait. Cast thy bread upon the water exactly harmo nizes with "Loosen it."

Luke 16 :9: "And I say unto you, make unto your selves friends of the mammon of unrighteousness; that when ye fail they may receive you into everlasting habita tions."

Literally the statement would nullify all the teaching of Jesus, and it is simply amazing that the so-called Chris tian world has so largely ig-nored it. However, a few critics from the orthodox ranks, not being at all satisfied with the rendering, have tried, in various ways, to recon cile the paradox, and to that end several pamphlets may be found in the theological departments of our colleges and universities.

Here is the explanation by a Greek scholar:

"Make unto your self *other* friends than those who worship the mammon of unrighteousness," etc.

Accenting the New Testament error, without question accounts for the great anxiety shown by churches of all denominations to secure the financial support of the wealthy, whether they be vital Christians, in belief, or nominally so. Proof of which may be seen in the end of the world, or age, nominally dominated by so-called Christianity.

Many worshipers of the mammon of unrighteousness exhibited much more horror over the destruction of costly cathedrals by the Huns than they did at the rape of women and slaughter of children by the Germans in Belgium, or murders by the sinking of the Lusitania.

Nothing can survive this "Day of Judgment" except it be founded upon the Truth, which liveth and reigneth forevermore.

38

JOSHUA COMMANDS THE SUN
AND MOON TO STAND STILL

IN Physiological Chart the solar plexus, a round body of tissue ganglion, may be plainly seen. Attached to the SUN (center) is a body called semi-lunar gan

glion (half moon), which is attached to the vertebra and spinal cord.   A median line (across the center of body) will divide these organs, half above the line, half below. The upper halves of the sun and moon vibrate for spir itual man and the lower half for *natural,* or animal man.

"There is a natural and a spiritual body."-Paul.

Now Joshua, the seed, on its way to the pineal gland is made to say, "Sun, stand thou still on Gibeon."

Gibeon means a mound or elevation. So the seed (Joshua, a fish), commands the animal vibration of *solar* (sun) plexus to stand still, *i.e.,* cease to continue to domi nate the spiritual forces, "while I slay my enemies" that is, the animal blood that predominates in carnal thought.

"And thou moon in the valley of Ajalon."

Ajalon means a "valley in Bethlehem," says a Bible dictionary.

Bethlehem-the house of bread: the *seed* is the bread.

Whoever conquers sex desire commands the sun and moon to stand still.

Who can do this?

"With man it is impossible, but with God all things are possible." Matt. 19th chapter.

Therefore, all can succeed by asking help from the "Most High."

. A cloud of witnesses may be found to substantiate the statement made above that the sun and moori in the Joshua story refer to the solar plexus and semi-lunar gan glion.

Eph. in Hebrew is prefix to many words meaning the

centre or middle. It is defined in Smith's Bible Diction ary under the name Eph-ah, as "First in order of the sons of Midian, *i. e.,* strife or contention between Michael and Apollyon occurs in the center of the body where the ani mal continually fights the upper force that seeks tq lift up and regenerate the animal or natural man.

Ephah also means weight (measure or balance, Libra, the scales).

Again, E-phes-dammin, "boundary of animal blood." "I fought with wild beasts at Ephesus."-Paul.

Ephesians are the children of Ephesus, the solar plexus, therefore the seed. Paul the still small voice, or intuition, redeeming (lifting up).

The seeds constitute Paul's Epistle to the Ephesians.

Once more: "Eph-raim is joined to his idols; let him alone."

This epigram defines the physical man, "Dead in tres pass and sin"- one who cannot be awakened by reason ing with him.

THE MEANING OF GLORY

GLORY is derived from glow and ray-to illumine, to light.

Prof. Smiley, formerly teacher of Greek in Cor nell University, writes: "The body is a lamp and this oil (referring to the oil descending the spinal cord) is its illuminating fluid."

Prof. Smiley also says: "This oil, in Greek, is from the root letters X. P. !.-Chrism or Chri"-Greek for oil, or Christ. •• "The *Christ in you,* the hope (substance) of glory," or light.-Paul.

But, says Paul, "If ye have only *hoped* Christ, ye are

of all men most miserable."   Why?

For "Unless Christ be *raised* our preaching is vain." The *only* way to *raise* THIS oil is by the seed entering the spinal cord and lifting up the oil. "If I (Jesus, the seed) be lifted up, I will draw *all* men (se-men, or oil) unto me."

Thus is the command, "Give one-tenth (tithe) unto the Lord," obeyed.

"The *entrance* of *thy word* giveth light"; "The seed is the WORD."-Luke.

John, Johannes, or Ioannes, means OIL, also an oint ment, and "Came to bear witness of that *light.*" St. John 1 :6.

Again-"That the Father may be glorified in the Son." John 14:13.

"Father, the hour has come; glorify thy Son, that thy Son may glorify thee."

Lip service cannot glow-ray or glorify God, but the seed "which is Christ" (Paul), saved and lifted up, car ries illuminating oil to the Father, enters the optic in the thalamus and giveth light. "And the temple needs rio other light."

We feel sure that those who desire the whole truth in regard to the real meaning of "glory" and "glorify"

will esteem it their duty and privilege to read St. John, and especially verses 22 and 24 of the 17th Chapter; also 19th verse of the 21st Chapter.   .

The word Saint means a perfect person, or one who realizes that Perfection even as the Father is perfect. According to the teachings of Scripture, the *Only* way that perfection can be attained is by saving the seed and thus be "Born of God."

The ancient painters painted a halo or a "nimbus of gold-colored light," as Walt Whitman sang, about the head of the Madonna, the infant Jesus and many of the saints and prophets. Hence we infer that the idea of an illuminating oil prevailed all down the ages. •

The Greek epic of the vestal Virgins keeping the fire or light forever burning and the wise virgins with lamps filled with oil, bear witness to the cosmic belief that there is a *substance* in man that enlightens and redeems, if not destroyed by animal forces.

OUR' EVER-PRESENT HELP

"For who maketh thee to differ from another? And what hast thou that thou *didst not receive?* Now if thou didst receive it, why dost thou glory, as if thou hadst not received it?"

"What I Know ye not that your body is the temple of the Holy Ghost which is *in you,* which ye have of God, and ye are not your own?"

"For ye are *bought with a price,* " etc. See "Give one tenth to the Lord," etc.

"Is not my help *in me?* And is wisdom driven quite from me?" Job 6 :13.

"Send the help from the *sanctuary,* and strengthen thee *out of* Zion."
(See explanation of these terms in glossary.)

"Our soul waiteth for the Lord; he is our help and our shield."

"God is our refuge and strength, a *very present* help in trouble."

•

"I will lift up mine eyes unto the hills, or mountains, from whence
cometh my help." "Mount of the Lord," the upper brain, "Most High."

THE TEMPLE OF GOD

"Know ye not that ye are the temple of God and that the spirit of
God dwelleth in you? If any man defile the temple of God, him shall
God destroy; for the temple of God is holy, which temple ye are." Man
defiles the temple by .preventing the seed (the *word)* from going up, or
returning to the upper brain, the cerebrum. In short, he eats of the fruit
of the tree of life, and there fore it cannot arise or return to the Kingdom, the optic thalamus, ana become the "Light in the chamber," where
it may "Cleanse from all sin."

He that overcometh (does not eat or destroy the seed, allows it "to
remain in him") "I will give to eat of the tree of life in the *"Father's Kingdom. "* See Lord's Supper.   •

The tree of life is the Vagus nerve (pneumogastric) and its branches.
(See article on Vagus nerve.)

Whose branches, or nerves, are called Nazareth, which is Greek for
shoot, sprout or twigs-little branches; hence, "Jesus of Nazareth, whom
thou persecuteth."

Jesus, the seed, thus speaks to Saul, who, after con version, no longer
used "S" (Schin or sin), but substi tuted "P," speech or "going forth, radiating," and thus became Paul the preacher.

Paul means "small" and refers to the seed itself. After the crucifixion
of Jesus (the seed) , the parable makes another seed take the place of the
first-born, and thus says, "I was born out of time."

SAUL OF TARSUS

Tarsus means "foot." Pisces, the fishes, are repre sented by the feet. In regard to "small," read the par- able of the "mustard seed."

"IN MY KINGDOM,,

"He that is born in thy house shall not be thine heir, but he that cometh forth out of *thine own bowels* shall be thine heir."

"She that is desolate hath many more children than she that hath an husband."

Here is proof that in the regeneration, that is, the plan of salvation *above* the solar plexus, there is no

marrying nor *giving* in marriage, for male and female are the same. Both have the same manger or WOMB, in man, both the same Ida and Pingala, or Joseph and Mary; and the same pneumogastric nerve that brings down the same Holy Ghost-breath-that conceives the seed, Jesus. Hence, Peter reads thus: "Born not of corruptible seed but of incorruptible; the Word of God." So, then, male and female in the new order MUST WORK OUT THEIR OWN SALVATION, the sav

ing seed that is in each separate body.

No sex reform, no physical contact-"Thou shalt not touch it"-Genesis; no effort to "climb up some other way" is tolerated, in the GREAT *TEXT* BOOK OF PHYSIOLOGY, THE HOLY BIBLE, or *whole book*.

THE BELOVED CATHOLIC PRIEST

Father John A. Ryan lays it down as "a fundamental ethical principle" that sexual intercourse for any other object than procreation is unnatural and "a perversion of the generative faculty on exactly the same moral level as the practice of the solitary vice."

"THE TREE OF LIFE"

The branches of the Vagus, or pneumogastric nerve, which extend to lungs and stomach, are called the "Tree of Life."

The oil or substance that flows down the plexus of nerves that branch off from the main nerve is deposited in the manger (the nun) or mouth of the fish, and forms a seed or *fruit* of the tree. This seed, being formed of the Esse of God, is called the Son of God, also the Son of Man that has "Power *in* earth (the body) to forgive sins. This seed says, "I am the way, the truth and the life"-hence the "Tree of Life."

THE ONLY CAUSE OF OLD AGE

Youth, strength and health depend entirely upon the automatic action of the blood which deposits the ma terial (itself) formed from the Esse, or substance called air, the breath of God, and the residue (ashes) of food, the mineral salts, and deposits it in the upper chamber, the cerebrum (Most High), the hallowed or hollowed place. (See fatted calf or Kaph.)

The secretions descending from this fat, oil the place of the secretions, build and sustain the entire bodily struc ture. But, if a certain amount, "one-tenth," is not re turned, the reservoir becomes depleted day by day until the deficiency, or sin *(i.e.,* falling short) causes weak ness, decrepitude, etc., which we, in our ignorance, have called "old age."

The Bible tells the cause and the remedy, thus: "The wages of sin is *death."*

But, "His delight is in the law of the Lord," *then:* "He shall be like a tree planted by the river of waters that bringeth forth its fruit in its season; but his leaf also shall *not wither,* and whatsoever he doeth shall *prosper."* .

There is one' cause of old age and one only: wasting the LIFE FORCE, the gray matter of the brain, the SEED, the WORD of God, which, if *saved,* results in "THE WORD MADE FLESH."

When people say unto you, "Lo l here," or "Lo I there

is the cause of old age," believe them not, for the cause of old age is within YOU.

SAMSON OR SAM SUN

The letter S in Hebrew is the 15th of the alphabet, and symbolizes the great dragon, the Great Dragon of the Threshold. In Hebrew it is Samech. The stomach is also symbolical of this letter. Here, also, is the Solar Plexus, the Sun Center or Son. Likewise, the physical power of the mind is centered here, the desire for Ani mal vibration, the "things thy soul lusteth after."

Samson, in Smith's Bible Dictionary, also means "Sun like, strong, distinguished."

Gaza simply means the "strong," or "strong city." Delilah means "weak, feeble," or "to pine with desire,"

and the symbolism is wrought into the form of a woman that tempted Samson, to destroy his strength by yielding to desire, or Delilah.

After sufficient time had elapsed in which material for a new seed could descend (as in the case of Hiram Abiff, in Freemasonry), Samson, through prayer, was able to save the seed, and was then spiritually strong, thus giving

him strength to tear down the Strong City of Gaza, or "Carry away the pillars of Gaza."

The reader is urged to study carefully the 13th Chapter of Judges to the 16th.

The story of the birth of Jesus and the warnings and prophecies concerning Samson are almost identical. He is even called "A Nazarite," which means, in Hebrew, "One consecrated to God."

In the story of Samson we read how he went down to, Etam. In Smith's Bible Dictionary we find that, in Hebrew, Etam means "A place of ravenous beasts." In this place was a high cliff or lofty rock which led down into a chasm or cleft where Samson went. Going down into this chasm, or place of ravenous beasts, is represented in Physiology by the vital fluid in the spinal cord going down into the seminal vesicles.

ISAIAH 31 :7

"For in that day every man shall cast away his idols of silver and his idols of gold, which your own hands have made unto you for a sin."

ISAIAH 28 :7-8

"But they also have erred through wine, and through strong drink are out of the way; the priest and the prophet have erred through strong drink, they are swallowed up of wine, they are out of the way through strong drink; they err in vision, they stumble in judgment. For all tables are full of vomit and filthiness, so that there is no place clean."

REVELATION, 22D CHAPTER, VERSES 1, 2

"And he showed me a pure river of water (spinal cord) flowing out of the throne of God (brain), and the Lamb (optic thalamus). "In the midst of the street of it and on either side of the river (both sides) was there the tree of life (pneumogastric nerve), which bare twelve manner of fruits, and yielded *her* fruit *every month* (seed every moon), and the leaves of the tree were (are) for the healing of the nations"-people.

The Indians, in their legend of the "Four trines within the Grand Symbol," call the solar plexus the "seed pod."

"BETWEEN TWO THIEVES"

The words "thief" and "steal" both mean "to operate in secret." Many things may be done in secret that are good, thus: "Give thine alms in secret"; "Let not thy left hand know what thy right hand doeth."

There is a wide difference between the original mean ing of words and their common application.

The pineal gland and pituitary body secrete the positive and negative substance along nerves that cross in the medulla, and the seed is cruci-fied between them, and the oil set free ascends to the pineal gland which is made to say: "Lord, remember me when thou cometh into thy king-dom."

Now, as th·e·fluids of the two glands had united and were ascending up the one on the "Right hand of the Father," the central eye, it would naturally say, "This day (now) shalt thou be with me in paradise."

He who spoke and he who replied were one and the same.

"MY YOKE IS EASY AND MY BURDEN IS LIGHT"

YoKE: To cross or bind. Oxen were yoked about the neck.

The nerves from the pituitary and pineal gland unite, and are thus bound together or yoked in the medulla oblongata ("Place of the Skull") and form a Cross.

In regeneration, when the seed crosses in the regular, automatic manner as the plan of salvation designed that

it should, the cervical, or neck, functions properly, and the soreness and uneasy feeling so prevalent in all who lead the animal or carnal life, which is "At enmity to God," or the spiritual life, often experience, and complain of, as every physician will testify.

Burden simply means that which is carried, not neces sarily some-thing heavy or tiresome.

The seed (any of the characters in Scripture) absorbs and carries the precious oil that flows down the spinal cord-the *"strait,"* up to the cross (yoke), where the "Cup" (cover of minerals) is "removed," which frees the precious oil. This illuminating substance then enters the

optic and "Giveth light to all that are in the house," or the chamber, the thalamus.

Thus does the redeeming seed truly say, "My burden is light," or illumination.

Paul bears witness thus: "The Christ (oil) in you, the hope of glory"-Glow-ray. Also, "Unless Christ be *raised* then is our preaching vain."

DORMANT BRAIN CELLS

In every brain there are countless dormant brain cells, waiting for the coming of the Air Age, the Bridegroom or the recognition of the "Christ in the flesh," that will quicken them into activity-i.e., resurrect them.

Everywhere there is evidence of the awakening of dormant brain cells. Spiritual phenomena, multiple per sonality, mental telepathy and kindred manifestations are explainable upon the hypothesis that dormant brain cells may be made to bloom and thus operate according to new concepts.

We know that there are many millions of dormant brain cells in the cerebrum, especially in the "Most High" portion, the seat of spiritual faculties; or, we may say, the key, which, when touched with the vital fluid set free, "Cast on the waters" and "Lifted up" through the process of physical regeneration, completes the at-one-ment with the Ego, whose indwelling place is the cerebellum. And then the statement, "I and the Father are One," becomes living thunder and flaming light from Sinai, instead of a popular epigram with no vital meaning.

The dormant brain cells may be likened to a flower yet in the bud; but when the substance that is required for their completion reaches them, the modus operandi of the plan of salvation, the buds open, or unfold, and then vibrate at the rate that causes the realization of the New Birth-the "Birth from above."

"He that is born of God will not sin, for *his seed*
remaineth in him."

And thus spake Paul: "We shall be changed in the twinkling of an *Eye"-not eyes-but* the optic thalamus, the "single," or perfected eye. See chart.

(

CHILDREN

Child means young, not aged.

"Children of Israel, or "warriors of God." See Smith's Bible Dictionary. There is not now, nor was there ever a geographical, historical land or nation called Israel. The name originated in secret or sacred books which are *not* historical or *outward,* but secret or *inward.*

The seeds that were saved every 29¼ days were called the "warriors of God."

"Suffer little children to come unto me, and forbid them not, for of such is the kingdom of heaven."

The seed is small.

"The kingdom of heaven is likened unto a mustard seed." •

The seed of all seeds, Jesus, the first seed, asks that other seeds might also be saved, for the seeds, saved and raised to the pineal gland, return to the heaven from which they came.

"Whosoever shall not receive the kingdom of God as a little child, he shall not enter therein."

The lion (animal force) (see Daniel in the lion's den) and the lamb (innocence, or spiritual concept) make at-one-ment (shall lie down together), and "A little child (seed) shall lead them," which means that the seed will carry up one-tenth of the descending fluid in the spinal cord (the great *strait)* to the Father, thus giving tithes to the Lord.

THE PSALMS OF DAVID

David is "Beloved of God"-psalm, "Praise, or hymn."

David is the seed, speaking, praising the source of its being and asking continually that its enemy, the carnal man, be destroyed.

"And David said to Gad, I am in a great *strait,* let me fall into the hands of the Lord and not in the hands of man."

The hands of man refers to the first man, Adam, or ani-mal desire. The strait is the spinal cord-"The strait and narrow way that leads to life eternal."

Gad refers to the tribe of Aries, the ram-the head

ruled by the brain substance-the OR, the Lord, or "Lord God from heaven."

"Jonathan-the praise of Jehovah." T, or Tav, in Hebrew, means a cross.

H, from Heth, means spiritual perception.

So Jonathan is a symbol of John, the baptizing fluid (oil) that de-scends from the upper brain that has been lifted by the seed (David), just as John, in the New Testament, was lifted up by Jesus after the baptism. "HE THAT RULETH HIS OWN SPIRIT

(SELF) IS GREATER THAN HE THAT TAKETH A CITY"

"If a man cannot rule his own house, how can he take care of the church of God?"

The Ego resides in and operates from the cerebellum, a house or beth, and is in direct communication with the upper brain, the FA-THER, not only by means of the connective tissue partition of ganglia, but also by the wondrous *lever,* the pineal gland, the "Root and the stem of Jesse." Jesse means "a traveler from Bethlehem" the very same as Je-sus, the seed.

The pneumogastric nerve also commences in the me dulla oblon-gata, against the cerebellum, and reaches down to the plexus, branches, in Bethlehem.

The thoughts of the Ego in its home in the cerebellum (called "heart" by the Greeks-"As a man thinketh in his heart so is he") may operate in the lower or Adam man, or in the "Lord God from heaven" realm.

This operation is·clearly and startlingly set forth in the ancient, thrice-told parable of the prodigal son, who *thought* it best to take his portion or *substance* and waste, or "eat it," in riotous living. The Ego thus ate of the fruit or bread of the tree of life, so that he did not rule or master himself. The natural sequence to this failure is a deficiency or wasting away of the gray matter of the brain, for the seed that should *lift up* one-tenth (tithe) every 29 _ ½ days has been eaten in Egypt and Sodom, "Where our Lord was also crucified." "For he that eateth and drinketh unworthily, eateth and drinketh dam nation to himself, not discerning the Lord's body."

In order to be able to *take* care of the house of God "Your body is the temple (house or church) of God," one must return a portion to the brain in the "Only way whereby he may be saved, Jesus Christed and crucified" the seed carried up the "Strait and narrow way," and cross-ified at the "place of the skull."

"AND ENOCH WALKED WITH GOD AND WAS N:OT, FOR GOD TOOK HIM"

"Enoch" is·Hebrew for initiation, and "Hebrew" means to Passover.   (See "Crossing Jordan," or "Crucifixion.") "Elijah went up in a chariot of fire."   Elijah means
the same as Jesus.

"Elijah's mantle fell on Elisha." Elisha represents the material for the next seed. "Mantle" means the same as cover or cup; "Father, remove this cup from me."

"The latchet of whose shoes I am not worthy to un loose." Mantle, cup, latchet, and shoes all refer to some thing that *covers.*

The record states that when Jesus was born he was "Put in swaddling clothes," or covered. The mineral salts in the medulla oblongata, through which the pineal and pituitary fluids flow on the way down the Ida and Pingala nerves, carry enough of the mineral salts to form the crust or seed that protects the "Precious Oint ment" that is finally re leased when the seed goes over the crossed Ida and Pingala, at Golgotha. Hence, "Father remove this cup (cover) from me."

Again, the "mantle that fell on Elisha" was this same cup or swad dling cloth that is represented by "As I go so will I come again." Who? This *same* Jesus, or "Elisha-Elijah.

"I am the resurrection and the life."

Moses represents the seed, also, found in an ark.

"To Abraham and his seed was the *promise* given, and to *thy* seed, which is Christ."-Paul.

"Whom do men say that I the Son of man am?

"And they said, Some say that thou are John the Bap tist, some Elias, and others, Jeremiah, or one of the prophets"-i.e., resurrected seeds.

God-Man: The Word Made Flesh

OM MANI PADME HUM

The Jewel in the Lotus

The lotus flower is the cerebrum, whose convolutions or petals re ceive all vibrations from without and are transmitted to the mechanism within, there to be trans lated into terms of the senses. Dew-drops from the boundless sea of the Virgin Mary, the tender mother, glisten on its perfumed petals, while they reflect the golden glory of the spiritual sun.

Countless thousands of these wondrous petals lie tightly closed in the cerebrum of the average person. Sad to relate, there are many, many people in whom the lotus petals have atrophied, died and decayed. Then the asy lum or the institution for the feeble minded claims them.

The Optic within the Thalamus is the heart, the fair jewel within the lotus bud. It is the stone the builders rejected.

The spinal cord is the stem of the lotus, a filament from which reaches down into the slime of the asphalt bed.

The Kundalini fire within the sacred plexus is the Bride of the Lotus, Lot's wife who looked back and became a pillar of salt.

As the dark and slimy bed conceals the quintessence of richness which fertilizes the lotus, and causes it to bud, so the vibrations from the sun above impinge upon this wonderful bud, and the force from above and the force from beneath, meeting in that wondrous heart of the lotus, causes all those beautiful petals to unfold, and lo I its heart lies bare to the universe.

And thus in you and I, when that quintessence of rich ness is kept within the body-when it is not "wasted in riotous living"-ascends the spinal cord, rising ever higher and higher until at last it reaches the heart of the lotus, the optic thalamus, vivifying it, revealing it, a glow ing, scintillating jewel reflecting the light of the Logos Himself and its petals wide open to receive vibrations which translate into the music of the spheres-and once again a lotus has bloomed.

When a human lotus blooms it is said that all nature thrills with gladness and thanksgiving.

THE HUMAN AUTOMOBILE

Man never invented anything. There is no *new* thing.

Within the "Fearfully and wonderfully made" human machine are the vestigial multiple forms conceived in the Infinite Mind, the prototypes of all things; and when the "Spirit in m n," the Ego, receives understanding from the "wisdom of the Almighty," it operates on the canvas of life before it, the plane of expression and form, shapes machines, and the factories of a transient commercialism which serve their day like a child's toy, then go into the discard and dis"appear. One day the coach and four-in hand, the next day the locomotive. Then man springs upon an automobile and drives it until the axles blaze and the spaces shrivel behind him.

Tomorrow he leaves earth behind and climbs the etheric terraces, peering into the unknown as if searching for the portals of some Celestial City.

The cerebellum is the chauffeur's seat, the pineal gland the lever, the cerebrum the gasoline tank (woe be to him who is out of oil}, the solar plexus is the speedometer, and the spinal cord is the passageway from the oil tank. The individual can run his automobile carefully, wisely,

at just the right speed, and with common sense. He can lose control and try to climb a telegraph pole, or go over an embankment. If he or she is a careful driver and looks to the well-being of his machine, he would be care ful to have his steering gear in perfect order. If he found his machine had a hole in the gas tank and that the gas was being' wasted, he would hasten to have it repaired. Does he • ever even think of the oil tank in his own body?

THE HUMAN THERMOMETER

The spinal cord may be likened to a thermometer. The lower part of the vertebrae, the Dead Sea, or the Lake of Asphaltum (Cauda Equina) is the congealed mercury or quicksilver, which may be refined (melted) or raised by heat.

When seeds have been saved so that that body becomes purified, the rate of its vibration has been changed, and at the proper time the wonderful Kundalini, the serpent fire, is released and rises to the top of the cord, going into the head and out through the door of Brahm-which is between the sutures. The mercury thus rises to the 33rd degree and goes over the top, reaching the *shade* or shadow of the Most High; 3 times 3 equals 9; thus 90 degrees in the *shade.*

THE PNEUMOGASTRIC OR VAGUS NERVE OR TREE AND HOLY GHOST

This wonderful nerve is the largest bundle of nerve fibers in the body. It is truly a Tree of Life, and its branches distribute the Holy Breath, essence, or *Ghost,* to lungs and solar plexus.

The breath, speaking from the natural body, is the air breathed into the lungs via the branches of trachea (Greek for rough), commonly termed wind-pipe.

For further information about the breath or *air* see "Turning water into wine." But the office of the pneu mogastric *tree* is to conduct and properly distribute the "Holy Ghost," the highly refined substance, a first potency of the breath that "God breathed into man."

When this breath is breathed into the body, about the age of twelve, and unites with the two different potencies of creative ".substance" that descends from the "Most High," via the pineal gland, Joseph (or increase), and also through the pituitary gland, Mar-y (pure fluid-water) that have descended the two wonder nerves, extensions of pineal gland and pituitary body, one on each side of the spinal cord, and cross this great Strait between the 12th dorsal vertebra, "in Egypt where our Lord was also crucified" ; thence united, they go up to the semi lunar ganglio, a *little space* (see chart), thence into the *manger* in Bethlehem. Here the Divine Drama is en acted and "Jesus is conceived of the Holy Ghost"-the whole breath, coming down the pneumogastric tree or nerve.

Pneumo means breath. Breath in Greek is ghost.

I

THE SON OF MAN

"Know ye not that the Son of man hath power *in* earth to forgive sins?"

Who is the Son of man?

"The seed (or word) is the Son of man."

Again, Revelation 19 :13-"And his name is called the WORD OF GOD."

REGENERATION

"Ye who' have followed (disciple is a follower) me in the regenera-tion. "Read entire chapter of Matthew 19. "Sell or exchange what thou hast and give *to the poor. "* Return one-tenth of the descending substance to the poor pineal gla,nd, the central eye and the upper brain that is slowly but surely wasting away-therefore get

ting poorer every day. Matt. 19.

How can this poverty be prevented? See Matt. 19. "With *man•* (car-nal or Adam-of earth, earthy), it is impossible, but with *God all* things are possible."

How shall we come in touch with God and realize our power-i.e., to be perfect, even as our Father in heaven 1s perfect?

Answer: "When ye pray for anything, *know* that ye have it *now. "*

This means that we recognize that all things exist *now* and that the *upper brain,* the Most High, the great reser voir of "enduring substance" (Paul) will give to the Ego, who resides in the cerebellum (see chart), whatso ever it asks, because the Ego RECOGNIZED the *reality* of the "Secret place of the MOST HIGH."

There are four brains in the human body. The cere brum, the cere-bellum, the medulla oblongata, and the solar plexus.

The Pingala nerve corresponds to the right sympathetic system; the Ida, to the left sympathetic system.

Sushumna passes from the terminus of the spinal cord to the top of the cranium.

"The spino-olivary fasciculus is a small tract, triangular in section, which runs on the surface of the cord and just lateral to the anterior roots of the spinal nerves. This is connected with the Dorsal Spino-cere-bellar Fasciculus.

The latter conveys non-sensory sympathetic impulses re ceived from the viscera. In the dorsal part of this nerve is a small strand of fibers called the spinal vestibular tract which rises in the *lumbar-sacral* region of the cord." Santee. We can easily see the connection between these nerves. The olivary of course has to do with the dis tribution of the oil and we know that the sacral ganglion is connected with the genitals.

"Fibers of the cerebrum concerned with the *higher* psy chic functions of the brain become medullated gradually, year after year, keeping pace with the mental develop ment, and the process of medullation is not completed until late in life."-Kaes.

There is a central canal within the spinal cord. That which is within this canal is of a substance more like steam or gas than anything else.

"AS A MAN THINKETH IN HIS HEART SO IS HE"

HOUGHT is the creative power in the universe. Universal intelligence, operating as thought, sprang' forth, "Spirit-sandalled and shod," at the

appointed time and in the appointed place, and Lo! the planet e,arth, man's sorrowful star, became manifest.

Earth is man's sorrowful star for the reason that only by means of trouble and pain does humanity learn its lessons. '

Spirit, manifesting on earth, uses earth as a negative pole, in order that the personality may grow. The min eral, vegetable and animal kingdoms use earth in much the same way. The earth is one plane of manifestation.

How can a man *think* in his *heart?*

The organ that divides blood was called by the ancients "dividing pump"-not heart. The real heart is the cere bellum and was so named by the Greeks and is the seat of thought.

Madame Blavatsky says, in the Secret Doctrine, that the cerebellum contains all, being the seat of intelligence. The thinker, the individual or "man who never dies," has his home, therefore, in the cerebellum, under the

shadow of the Almighty.

Read what the writer of the 91st Psalm has to say about this: "He that dwelleth in the secret place of the Most High shall abide under the shadow of the Al mighty."

Secret (secretion, oil or ointment) place of the Most High-is that place where the secretion of oil or ointment is found. In the Bible we see so many references to oil anointing, secret, secretions, etc.

This plainly shows that the place of the Most High is the cerebrum, that portion of the anatomy of man whence comes the oil or ointment-the precious substance that

fructifies the brain of man and causes it to develop; it is that which nourishes the brain.

The abiding place of the Ego *is* "Under the shadow of the Almighty," since the cerebrum extends entirely over and around it.

And again the Psalmist says:

"He will cover thee with his pinions

and under his wings shalt thou take refuge."

The feathery convolutions which are plainly shown in the upper brain may be well compared to the feathers of a bird. The "Voice of the Silence" speaks of the Ego resting "Under the wings of the Great Bird."

The upper brain is composed of highly specialized sub stance. It is a reservoir of God's creative compounds. It is that God-making material-the Kingdom of Heaven wherein all is found.

"Seek ye first the Kingdom of Heaven and all things shall be added unto you."

"The Kingdom of Heaven is within you." Heaven means "heaved up"-a high place.

The cerebrum is, then, the kingdom of heaven, for it is within us. By seeking it we draw from it the precious oil or ointment which shall nourish the brain and therefore cause it to grow and expand.

Certain parts of the brain cells are dormant. They are in a certain slow rate of motion or activity, and, therefore, answer to vibrations of their kind.

Let us suppose, for example, that little cell in the brain is composed of spirallae, spirals of nerves, seven sets of which can be seen by the trained occultist.

In a person of low intelligence only three or four of these spirallae will be found to be active, while the man who is already working along the line of regeneration living the life of self-sacrifice, will show five and six in active operation.

The higher and more lofty the *quality* of the thought, the finer or higher the vibration. Just as the vibration of the ether strikes upon the tympanum of the ear and pro duces sound-so are the spirallae of the brain cells oper ated upon by the fingers of the heavenly man, *when* the Kingdom is sought.

Thought, then, is a vibration, and as a·man thinks so does he vibrate his brain cells.

How many people really think?

The war has done more to wake people up and set them to thinking than anything else ever could have done. It has started that process,in many people-it has forced them to think.

Thought is a particular development of ideas, some thing entirely apart from the "hit-or-miss," "ramshackle" process w ich was supposed to be thought. .

Let us begin to think; let us *choose* the material from which we shall build our temples-the temple of the **"Liv** ing God."

The process that the average man calls thought is not consecutive thinking. God hasten the day when people will realize that all that is, has been or will be, is the re sult of thought.

Thought is both creative and destructive.

Not only are we making our bodies now, but we are making those which we shall wear in the future. .

By the future I mean when the individual is reincar nated.

A great thinker has said: "Know this mighty fact, the soul is but the fruitage of thought tinctured and tarnished with the emotions, passions and desires of the flesh.11

First, as regards the physical body. Thought selects the food by which the body is nourished. The cells of the body are being constantly de stroyed and rebuilt. The purest food possible to obtain will construct a pure body. Vegetables, fruits and grains are of much finer construc tion than flesh, and hence can vibrate to much higher rates of motion.

Flesh is decaying animal matter and is detrimental to the highest de velopment of man. Much flesh eating thor oughly coarsens the body, and the marks of his calling are stamped on the face of the butcher.

Another example is that of a man who drinks. Alco hol brings about exactly the same result. The body can not respond to any of the higher vibrations.

Just as surely as the note you strike on the piano must produce a cer tain tone, just so surely will your body

answer to the same rate of vibration around it that it vibrates to in itself.

The high cost of flesh food during the war has been a blessing in dis guise, for it was the only means whereby people could be brought to re alize that they could still *live* if they never ate meat. Then, after a time, they will begin to realize that they can enjoy much better health without it.

If you wished to do a fine, delicate piece of work, you would not use coarse or unwieldy instruments in doing it.

Just as true is it that the vehicle of the spirit-Solo mon's Temple-must be delicately and finely constructed.

The body must be kept scrupulously clean and be given sufficient exercise.

If your body is not satisfactory to you, it is because you have indulged in thoughts that have marred its con struction.

It is never too late to do *something* toward the recon
struction and regeneration of the body.
Start *NOW.*

The physical man is made up of twelve divisions, *i. e.,* bone man, muscular man, nerve man, etc.   These are all constructed with a certain cell salt or mineral as a base for each man or division of the body, see "Relation of the Mineral Salts of the Blood to the Signs of the Zodiac." Each cell of the body is a *living,* throbbing intelligence.

Each cell actually reaches out and grasps from out the water of life-'that living stream of blood that is the life of the body-just the material it needs in its construction. "The quality of the force·called into action in any king
dom determines the quality of the offspring."

You are directly responsible for each thought that occupies your brain.

The soul is the thought man and the emotional man that occupies the physical bodies resembles it in form and feature. We do not here refer to the Spiritual Ego.

If, then, our thoughts build our bodies, what thoughts are the cell lives of the body filled with? We must natur ally see that they are, in vast numbers, filled with thoughts of fear, strife and blood. Fears of microbes,

disease, poverty, the neighbors, the weather, the night air, the dark, burglars, etc., etc.

Eternal strife for wealth, position and power, for ma terial benefits. Benefits, so-called.

All this brings about war-the cell life gorged with blood, calling for the blood of its brothers.

Is not the cause of the war clear?

Do not thoughts pollute the very air? Is it not true that our thoughts affect those around us? What about the cells th:h we throw off from our bodies every minute

-cells that we have built and that are impregnated with our thoughts?

What is the matter with the people in the world? For there is nothing the matter with the world itself.

Each cell, then, that we throw off from our bodies, hour by hour and day by day, bears the stamp of our thoughts upon it. These go to make up the record of our lives, which those whose eyes are opened can read. In occultism this is called the Akashic record.

Then each man is the recording angel.

"Like attracts like." Birds of a feather flock to gether." These are trite sayings.

We see, then, that the cellular construction and fineness of the tissues of the physical man is determined by the character of the thoughts we store away in them.

The prodigal son wasted his substance in riotous living. His thoughts were turned toward the indulgence of the lower passions, like the rich young man who went away sorrowful because he had many possessions. Therefore the precious substance, the oil or ointment, the elixir of life, was sold for a mess of pottage. The seed, Jesus, or Christ, was not saved. If his thoughts had been pure and clean, the seed would have reached the cerebellum and would have increased in power a thousand fold. They then would have become the anointed of the Lord would have received the oil or oinment. The prodigal would then have become the son "in whom the Father was well pleased."

- When the thoughts of the disciple are purified from every un-desirable thought-then he becomes the son **of** the Master for his thought flows like a river through the consciousness of his Lord.

His body has become transfigured, for each seed has become crucified and Christed. Each cell of his body has thrown off all its impurities and has become *white* in the blood of the lamb, for the blood of the lamb is as a crystal stream.

The process of regeneration causes the white corpuscles of the blood to overcome the preponderance of red, or Mars corpuscles.

Therefore the flesh becomes transparent-and he man ifests more and more of the Father-he is no longer man-but has become a God.

Paul says: "Now, then, are we the sons of God." "All things I have done ye can do, and greater."

As we go on living the regenerative life, the time comes when we no longer respond to any law within the physical realm, for all physical matter has been cast off from the body. "It is sown a material and is *raised* (because the seed has been raised-the rate of vibration has been raised) a *spiritual* body, and the Kingdom of Heaven has been attained.

"HE THAT OVERCOMETH"

The above sentence occurs nine times in Revelation.

To overcome a vice or habit means *to cease to do* it. In the Scriptures overcome is used to symbol the triumph of the Ego over sex or animal desire. It means the con quering of the carnal mind.

REVELATION 2, 7-"He that hath an ear, let him hear

what the Spirit saith unto the churches; To him that overcometh will I give to eat of the tree of life, which is in the midst of the paradise of God."

REVELATION 2, 11-"He that hath an ear, let him hear what the Spirit saith unto the churches; He that overcometh shall not be hurt of the second death." REVELATION 2, 17-"He that hath an ear, let him hear what the Spirit saith unto the churches; To him that overcometh will I give to eat of the hidden manna,

and I will give him a white stone, and in the stone a new name written, which no man knoweth saving he that receiveth it."

REVELATION _2, 26, 27-"And he. that overcometh, and keepeth my works unto the end, to him will I give power over the nations." "And he shall rule them with a rod of iron; as the vessels of a potter shall they be broken to shivers; even as I received of my Father. And I will give him the morning star."

REVELATION 3, *5-"He* that overcometh, the same shall

be clothed in white raiment; and I will .not blot out his name out of the book of life, but I will confess his name before my Father, and before his angels."

REVELATION 3, 12-"Him that overcometh will I make a pillar in the temple of my God, and he shall go no more out: and I will write upon him the name of my God, and the name of the city of my God, which is new Jerusalem, which cometh down out of heaven from my God: and I will write upon him my new name."

REVELATION 3, 21-"To him that overcometh will I grant to sit with me in my throne, even as I also overcame, and am set down with my Father in his throne."

REVELATION 21, 7-"He that overcometh shall inherit all things ; and I will be his God, and he shall be my son."

EXTRACT FROM "DISCOURSES FROM THE SPIRIT-WORLD

IT IS thought that Stephen Olin was First President of Wesleyan University.

"The inhabitants of the earth may look forward with joyful assurance that the time is approaching when heaven shall be manifest on earth in the glorious harmo nies that will everywhere greet the eye and cheer the heart. *As certain as the revolutions of time move for ward,* SO SURELY WILL THE DIVINE GLORY BE VISIBLY DISPLAYED AND ALL NATIONS SHALL BEHOLD AND ENJOY THE BLESSED NESS OF CELESTIAL *ILLUMINATION.* Such

being the future and happy result that awaits the earth and its inhabitants, how important, fellow mortal, is *your duty* to hasten on the grand consummation. Arise from your inactivity and dullness and *move forward* in obedi ence to the laws of your being. Let no excuse prevent the utmost development of your whole nature. Exercise all the powers of your mind and body with reference to the harmonial unfolding of yourself. Do what you can to assist others in the great work of spiritual and physical development. Learn from the volume of inspiration in the universe without, and let your spirit look within for still higher manifestations and *more refined* enjoyments.

CONSUMMATION 1927

HE reyolutionary planet Uranus will have com pleted·his seven years' journey through Pisces, and entered the sign Aries, representing the up-per brain,
in January, 1927.
The stars in their course
Are nearing the dawn of peace. The purpling mountain-tops
Of human love appear. Look! Listen!
Above the battle's din you may hear The anthem of "Peace on earth."
Good will to men is in the air.
Out from the curling mists of the Pacific Sea That twist and twine
Like things alive;
From the glory of the upclimbing clouds Of the morning, that spill their jewels On the grass and flowers ;
In the liquid notes of the shuttle-throated mocking bird That pours its rippling prayers
Into the ears of Deity;
F.rom the clean-trunked eucalypti,
From orange blossoms and pendant pepper bough; From the sweet-faced little children;
From the hearts of earnest men; From the souls of women-mothers;
From the planetary angles

And rising constellations; From the heavenly hosts that "Declare the glory of God";

From the inner sanctuary of cosmic law Wemay hear the song of Peace.

Peace comes!

Reach forth thy hands, brothers, sisters, Welcome thy Savior-Peace.

Offend her not I

Bow to the radiant queen I

We are so weary-

Yea, sick unto death-of war. Our Healer comes-

The Great Physician.

Let all rejoice and be glad.

Let us join the song, Peace unto Thee!

From the Seven Sacred Centers of regenerate human bodies; from the Secret Places of the Most High, where immortal Egos sit enthroned in the wondrous brain of man-the new Jerusalem-is heard the Divine Anthem. The music of the Spheres, out and out in realms of Cos mic Law, now becomes audible, and choruses with the re deemed and glori-fied earth.

Flowers bloom fresh in her footsteps;

The folds of her white garments are like "trailing clouds of glory." The co-operative commonwealth of humanity looms behind her. The bugles all sing truce along the.iron front of war.

Ironclads rust.

Airships climb and climb into the ether,

As if seeking the portals of the Celestial City. The trenches are cov-ered with grass.

Vines clamber over arsenals, Flowers bloom on deserted forts.

Soldiers become men at home, field, shop, firesides, Women love and children play.

"The ransomed of the Lord return And come to Zion---

With everlasting joy upon their heads." And all over and about

The air is full of the scent of flowers, And the trickling fall of fountains,

And free men and women have started on the Great Adventure To find God.

"And I saw a New Heaven and a New Earth,"

The old has passed away and the sun of righteousness arises with Healing in its beams.

THE END